Elgar Mo[...]

In the Bavarian Highlands

Edward Elgar's German Holidays in the 1890s

Peter Greaves
with original photographs by
Jean Greaves

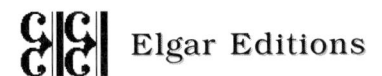

Elgar Editions

Published in Great Britain by

Elgar Editions

the publishing imprint of

Elgar Enterprises
20 High Street, Rickmansworth, Herts WD3 1ER
(e-mail : editions@elgar.org)

© Peter Greaves 2000

First Published : May 2000

All rights reserved.
No part of this publication may be reproduced, stored in a retrieval system,
or transmitted in any form or by any means, electronic or mechanical,
without the prior permission in writing of Elgar Enterprises.

This book is sold subject to the condition that it shall not,
by way of trade or otherwise, be lent, re-sold, hired out or otherwise circulated
in any form of binding or cover other than that in which it is published
without the publisher's prior consent and without a similar condition
including this condition being imposed on any subsequent purchaser.

British Library Cataloguing in Publication Data
A Catalogue record of this book
is available from the British Library

ISBN 0 9537082 1 7 (Elgar Editions)

Printed and bound in Great Britain by
Hobbs the Printers Limited,
Brunel Road, Totton, Hampshire

Frontispiece :   *Elgar's sketch of the drinking fountain by the Loretto chapels*
                   (see page 40).   *[Elgar Birthplace Museum/Elgar Will Trust]*

Contents

	Author's acknowledgements	iv
	Author's introduction	1
I	Ambitions and Preparations	3
II	Journeys to and from Bavaria	10
III	Munich	23
IV	Oberstdorf	33
V	Garmisch	43
VI	The Villa Bader, Karl Bader and the Slingsby-Bethells	61
VII	The Bavarian Highlands Music	75
Appendices		
A	Bibliography	91
B	List of Recordings	92
Index		94

The Author

Peter Greaves was educated at King Edward VII School, King's Lynn and at Goldsmiths' College, University of London. He also holds degrees from the Open University and the University of Leicester. He held senior positions in Luton high schools and was a member of the part-time staff of the Open University.

Together with his wife Jean, a keen photographer, who is responsible for the original illustrations in this book, he joined the Elgar Society in 1980, taking an active interest in its activities.

Acknowledgements

Grateful thanks are due to all the authors and their publishers who have given permission to quote from and refer to their works as listed in the bibliography.

Thanks are also due to Geoffrey Hodgkins for his advice and encouragement and to Ann Vernau for her editorial assistance. Similarly, I am most grateful to John Norris for his invaluable help and advice.

Finally, special thanks are due to a group of friends and relatives, without whom this book would not have been written : to my wife, Jean, who assisted and advised in the writing and took the original photographs; to Peter Adam and Martin Schöll, our friends in Garmisch, for their help and detective work in discovering the whereabouts of the Villa Bader and for supplying illustrations, documents and photographs; and last, but most importantly, my computer literate daughter and her husband, Elizabeth and Clive Makin, who word-processed the text and its several revisions, and also prepared the illustrations and maps.

Author's Introduction

Sir Edward Elgar's claim to fame as one of the greatest, if not *the* greatest of English composers, rests largely on the Enigma Variations, the oratorios (notably *The Dream of Gerontius*) and the great orchestral works of the early 1900s. Until the recent issues of recordings using orchestral accompaniments, *From the Bavarian Highlands*, the choral suite published in 1896, had been relatively neglected. Certainly there is a gap in the Elgarian literature concerning it. Little, if anything, has been specifically written about the 1890s holidays in Germany, especially Munich and Bavaria. This publication seeks to fill that void.

Since my wife and I joined the Elgar Society in the early 1980s, we have been enthusiastic followers of the various Elgar "trails": visits to places in which the composer lived and worked, places where he visited his friends and where he and his wife Alice spent their holidays have been made possible largely through the Society's activities. We found these experiences important as background to accompany the enjoyment of Elgar's music.

In 1984 we set out on an Elgar trail which resulted in this book. The brief references in the Elgar biographies to the Elgars' holidays in Germany fascinated us and we resolved to recreate for ourselves these same holidays: to enjoy the lovely areas in Bavaria, especially Garmisch and Oberstdorf, and to discover the present-day location of the Villa Bader in Garmisch, where Edward and Alice stayed as guests of the Slingsby-Bethells. The book documents this search, which was ultimately successful, and also our recreation of Edward and Alice's German holidays.

We hope that this and other information will guide Elgar enthusiasts in following yet another "trail" as we have done. At the same time they will experience the lovely region of Bavaria, and understand why Edward and Alice enjoyed their holidays there, returning several times in the 1890s.

Peter Greaves,
December 1999

Cover illustration of catalogue for Herkomer exhibition, 1885
[Courtesy Bushey Museum and Art Gallery]

Chapter One

Ambitions and Preparations

Edward Elgar had for many years longed to visit Germany. At the age of fifteen, the desire to become a composer was already strong, and he wanted to go to Germany where all the best musicians went to study. Years later, in May 1904, he told the interviewer from *The Strand Magazine* that he had hoped for a musical education. Indeed he had worked hard at learning German in preparation for attendance at Leipzig Conservatoire. In the end his tradesman father could not meet the costs and Elgar had to abandon any plans to go to Germany for this purpose.[1]

This frustration was somewhat relieved when in the autumn of 1882 he made plans for his first trip to Germany. He was to realise his dream of going to Leipzig at last, if only for a few weeks in the Christmas holidays, to hear all the music he possibly could, including productions of *Lohengrin* and *Tannhäuser*, as well as a concert performance of the Prelude to Act I of *Parsifal*. Edward was undoubtedly in sympathy with the prevailing good relationship between this country and Germany in the 1880s; and he also recognised during this decade the enviable musical advantages enjoyed by the Germanic peoples, which he glimpsed during his 1882 visit.[2]

One such benefit was the music of Wagner. The earliest evidence of this association with Wagner was at a concert of the Worcester Glee Club on 23 October 1876, for which he arranged the overture to *The Flying Dutchman*.[3] His friend, Hubert Leicester, recalled that at about

---

[1] See quotation from *The Strand Magazine* May 1904 p 538 in Moore, Jerrold Northrop: *Edward Elgar: A Creative Life* (Oxford University Press, 1984) p 55

[2] See also Young, Percy M: *Alice Elgar - Enigma of a Victorian Lady* (Dennis Dobson, 1978) p 111

[3] See Dennison, Peter: 'Elgar's Musical Apprenticeship' in *Elgar Studies* (Scolar Press, 1990) p 9

the same time Edward was playing music from the *Tannhäuser* overture on the organ. He was involved in Wagner's music again at the Three Choirs Festival when he was in the orchestra which played the march and chorus 'Hail bright abode' from Act II of *Tannhäuser*.

Although Elgar also played in William Stockley's orchestra in Birmingham when they performed some of the more popular Wagnerian excerpts, his experience of Wagner at this time grew mainly as a result of his attendance at the London concerts conducted by August Manns and Hans Richter.[4] On 3 March 1883 Manns conducted the memorial concert for Wagner who had died in Venice on 13 February. Elgar attended this concert and annotated his programme with highly appreciative comments.[5] Wagner's music was played often at the St James's Hall with Richter conducting. The latter included not only concert pieces and orchestral extracts from the operas but also operatic scenes in their entirety. Thus, on 23 May 1887, he conducted the 'Ride of the Valkyries' and the love scene from Act I of *Die Walküre*. Again, Elgar was present and annotated his programme. Then in 1889, the year of Edward's marriage to Alice Roberts and move to London, productions of Wagnerian opera became more frequent in the city and he saw several of these, including *Die Meistersinger* which in July 1889 he saw at Covent Garden no fewer than three times.

There is no doubting Elgar's desire to widen his Wagnerian musical experience. Most of the standard biographies detail this, thus also revealing the certainty that many of Edward's friends were aware of his ambitions.

Yet another influence, on Alice as well as Edward, was the appeal of new metaphorically romantic landscapes inspired by artists. For in the year 1891, during a particularly depressing period whilst living in London, they subscribed to a series of the hundred best pictures published by Charles Letts and Co. They made their own index of this fortnightly publication, each part containing six reproductions. It has been suggested that the Elgars, in common with many others of the aspiring middle classes in the late nineteenth century, were attracted

---

[4]   *ibid*

[5]   *ibid*

to artists' work depicting European holiday and tourist centres. One such area was Bavaria.[6]

A principal artistic exponent of Bavarian themes was Hubert von Herkomer[7] who was born in Waal, near Landsberg, on 26 May 1849 in a house now bearing a memorial name plaque. His parents had emigrated to America in 1851 but, after six years in Cleveland, Ohio, left the United States and settled in Southampton, England where, despite a family life of harsh poverty, Hubert was able to study at the local school of art and later at Munich Academy.[8]

Whilst in Munich, Herkomer developed a profound interest in the national origins of his family. In the spring of 1871, aged 22, he returned to Bavaria to spend six months in Garmisch, living among the peasants. Thereafter he visited Bavaria frequently, often for long periods. Although Herkomer always regarded himself as an English artist, his choice of a Bavarian subject 'After the Toil of the Day' (1873) for his first major exhibition painting in oil shows his divided national loyalties, even at the beginning of his career. For, although inspired by Bavaria and given a Bavarian setting, the style of 'After the Toil of the Day' owes much to Victorian rural idealism and portrays villagers returning home after the work day or reclining on benches which line the village street of Garmisch. Other Bavarian subjects followed: 'At Death's Door' (1876), a scene of a family awaiting a priest to administer the last rites to a dying relative;[9] 'Der Bittgang' (1877), a procession of peasants praying for a bountiful harvest; and 'Light, Life and Melody' (1879). The latter is a very large painting depicting a Bavarian scene. The subject is a bowling alley in a mountain bierhaus where the local people are listening to a zither player.

There were several other pictures shown that year with Bavarian themes : 'Weary' (1873) and 'Grandfather's Pet' (1880); 'Auf der Alm'

---

[6] Young, *op cit*, p 117

[7] The following passage is a development of an idea suggested in Young, *ibid*

[8] See Edwards, Lee M: 'Sir Hubert von Herkomer : English or German painter' in *Sir Hubert Herkomer, a Catalogue of the Centenary exhibition celebrating the Landsberg Mutterturm* (1988) p 22

[9] Edwards, *op cit*, p 34

After the Toil of Day by Hubert Herkomer
[Private Collection]

(1879), a study of Bavarian women at work in the mountain pastures; and 'Words of Comfort' (1883), an old woman and a girl seated under the eaves of a Bavarian-type chalet. But generally it was in the Grosvenor Gallery exhibitions that Herkomer's work attracted most attention and, among many others that she attended, these afforded Alice much pleasure. So her susceptibility to these Bavarian pictures, added to Edward's interest in Wagner's music, must have played no little part in their desire to journey to this lovely part of Germany.[10]

By the beginning of 1892, Edward and Alice Elgar had returned to Worcestershire and were living in Malvern Link in circumstances which made the prospect of a visit to Germany and Bavaria seem remote. At that time it would have involved a long journey by boat and railway of some 600 - 700 miles, lasting at least two, and possibly three, days.

---

[10] Young, *op cit*, p 118

Ambitions and Preparations

It is sometimes suggested that, in the last years of the 19th century, conservative Bavaria appealed to the 'well-heeled' Englishman as a holiday destination. Perhaps 'well-heeled' was a little over-optimistic as far as the Elgars were concerned at this time, though there cannot be any doubt where their aspirations lay, if not, as some would suggest, the wherewithal to realise them. Yet we must remember that, as Digby Hague-Holmes comments:[11]

> When it came to holidays, no one from the working or lower middle classes ever took a real break, and very few from even the upper middle classes would have ventured abroad for that purpose. And yet from the start of their marriage, the Elgars frequently travelled on the continent - usually first class, although they could ill afford it.

Nevertheless, the Elgars made a 'brave show' of keeping up with the Fittons and other friends who gathered at Forli to play, or listen to, music, especially the comparatively new works of Brahms and Grieg.[12] They had moved into Forli in Alexandra Road on 20 June 1891 on their return from the relatively unsuccessful sojourn in London at 51 Avonmore Road, West Kensington. Healthwise, Edward had spent a rather miserable year, a fair amount of the time ill in bed. He had suffered from a succession of eye, throat and dental problems.

However, over the New Year 1892 the Elgars were able to stay with the Bakers at Hasfield Court. Mr W M Baker was the Squire of Hasfield Court in Gloucestershire; he ultimately figured in the *Enigma Variations* (No 4) but, although his sister and wife did not, it was to them the Elgars owed most. Mrs Baker was far more bohemian in taste than most of Elgar's friends and probably had some understanding of Edward's ambitions. It was Miss Baker, the sister, however, who really went out of her way to help and befriend the Elgars.[13] She was a woman of great personal charm and character who had known Alice for many years. Alice had taken Edward to meet her old friend, Mary Frances Baker (affectionately known as Minnie) at Miss Baker's large house 'Covertside' in the hamlet of Hasfield, near Redmarley, before

---

[11]   Hague-Holmes, Digby: 'Elgar and the Class Society' in *The Elgar Society Journal*, January 1994 Vol 8 No 4 p 154

[12]   Young, *op cit*, p 111

[13]   Burley, Rosa and Carruthers, Frank C: *Edward Elgar - The Record of a Friendship* (Barrie and Jenkins, 1972) p 93

they were married in 1889. It was after this and other meetings, including the New Year invitation and visit, that, early in February, after Edward had suffered another bout of throat trouble and influenza, they went to Covertside to stay for a week with Minnie Baker. Edward soon established a friendly rapport with her, a measure of which was his invention of a nickname for her - 'The Mascotte', after the popular comic opera by Edmond Audran.[14]

Then shortly after came an invitation from Minnie, probably influenced by realising her friend Alice's reduced circumstances, to accompany her on a summer holiday. The journey would principally include Bayreuth for performances of the Wagner operas. Several years later Elgar was to tell 'Dorabella' that Minnie gave them a "splendid time". She undoubtedly made the German holiday a reality, although how much she was exactly responsible for financing it is not known.

So at last Edward was to realise one of his great ambitions, to see Wagner performed at Bayreuth, and there is no doubt that he had made careful preparation for the eagerly anticipated experience. He obtained printed analyses of *Meistersinger, Tristan* and *Parsifal*. Next he cross-referenced in detail every theme in the analysis to its correct page reference in the vocal scores.[15] Certainly, having seen *Tristan* in 1892, this opera exercised a spell over him and, as a result, similar preparations were made for the 1893 holiday; the second holiday in Germany in as many years, this time on their own resources with interest centred mainly on Garmisch and the Wagner Festival in Munich, the Musik Fest. On 1 June, the day before his 36th birthday, his own copy of the piano vocal score of Tristan arrived. In it he wrote:

> This Book contains the Height, - the Depth, - the Breadth, - the Sweetness, - the Sorrow, - the Best and the whole of the Best of This world and the Next.
> Edward Elgar.[16]

And throughout June he was revising and relearning his knowledge of the German language. The Elgars' arrangements were assisted by Rosa

---

[14] Moore, *op cit*, p 159

[15] *op cit*, p 164

[16] *op cit*, p 173

Ambitions and Preparations

Burley, who was able to supply them with a list of addresses which they could use to book rooms in which to stay.

For the second year running they would be absent for their daughter Carice's birthday, her third, and she would be sent with her nurse to stay with Minnie Baker. The Elgars had hoped to let Forli for the summer of 1893 while they were away, but this arrangement fell through, so the family plate was packed into a chest and looked after by Basil Nevinson.[17]

In 1894, Carice was left with Rosa Burley, and Elgar's precious violin 'Messer Nicolo' was left for safe keeping with the violin dealer, Hill of London. In its place a modern Chanot was taken as a travelling substitute. Again, in 1895, Rosa Burley was given charge of Carice but no other arrangements are recorded.

The 1897 holiday was arranged so suddenly that only the barest preparations and hurried packing were possible. It was not until 8 August that Edward decided that the Bavarian mountains were calling him. On 10 August, barely a month before the Hereford Three Choirs Festival was due to begin, Alice, having spent the previous day packing and "very busy", left with Edward on the 8.40 am train for London. She went to Cook's to fetch tickets whilst Edward visited Novello. Alice then oversaw the conveyance of luggage to Victoria before meeting Edward at "exactly the right moment at the Earl's Court Exhibition". They left Victoria at 9.50 pm for Queenborough and, on "a fine still night", embarked for Flushing (Vlissingen).[18]

---

[17] Collett, Pauline: *An Elgar Travelogue* (Thames Publishing, London, 1983) p 105

[18] Elgar, Alice: Diary entry for Tuesday 10 August 1897

Chapter Two

Journeys to and from Bavaria

All the Elgars' journeys to and from Bavaria in the 1890s were, of course, made by boat and railway train. Naturally, this dictated the routes followed and the places visited en route, as the maps of their journeys will show. Edward and Alice used the journeys to good effect, despite the limitations of rail travel, and visited a wide variety of places making mainly overnight stops.

But first they had to get across to the continent. Dover was the principal port of departure. This they first used on Monday 25 July 1892, having met their travelling companion, Minnie Baker, at Margate on 22 July; then again on 2 August 1893, having stayed overnight at the Castle Hotel; and finally in 1895. The sea crossing from Dover landed them in Ostend. In 1894, however, they travelled via Harwich, leaving on 31 July and arriving at the Hook of Holland the next day, while in 1897, having sailed from Queenborough, they disembarked at Flushing.

As the maps show, the return journeys were also by the Ostend-Dover sea crossing except in 1895, when they travelled home via Paris and

Beethoven's birthplace in Bonn
[J W Greaves]

Journeys to and from Bavaria

crossed from Dieppe on 11 September, before arriving in London about 7 pm. Alice recorded in her diary that this was "a lovely day".[1]

Landing at and departing from Ostend always seemed to dictate a stop-over in Cologne at the Hotel du Nord. This happened during the outward journeys in 1892, 1893 and 1895 (as well as in 1897 when they landed at Flushing), and for the return journeys in 1892, 1893, and 1897. An essential part of their visit to Cologne was their attendance at High Mass in the cathedral. The diaries tell us that they "wondered at Cologne Cathedral" and their visits are noted for most years on the outward and return journeys.

1892

Their 1892 journey is the most fully documented. As the map overleaf shows, having landed at Ostend they travelled via Cologne, Bonn, and Mainz to Bayreuth and then on to Nuremberg, Munich and Oberstdorf. On the way home they visited Lindau, Heidelberg, Cologne and Brussels.

After their stay in Cologne on the outward journey, the Elgars called in at Bonn and, despite Edward having one of his frequent headaches, they drove to Beethoven's birthplace in order to pay homage to the great composer.

Travelling on by Rhine river steamer, they arrived at Mainz (which they also visited in 1893) at 9.30 in the evening, and stayed at the Hotel Englischer-Hof. The next day, 27 July, they visited the Dom (cathedral) and also the museum to see the Gutenberg Bible. In Elgar's own words, they "firebranded around Mainz".[2] They left for Bayreuth at 12.40 pm, having found Mainz station "chaotic". However, after changing from a 2nd to a 1st class carriage, they eventually, in Alice's words, "dawdled on to Bayreuth", arriving some eleven hours later at 11.30 pm. They again found the station "chaotic" and their late arrival meant they had great difficulty in finding food. They stayed at 7 Ludwig Strasse for five days.

---

[1] Elgar, Alice: Diary entry for 11 September 1895

[2] Also quoted in Anderson, Robert: *Elgar* (Master Musicians Series, Dent, 1993) p 26

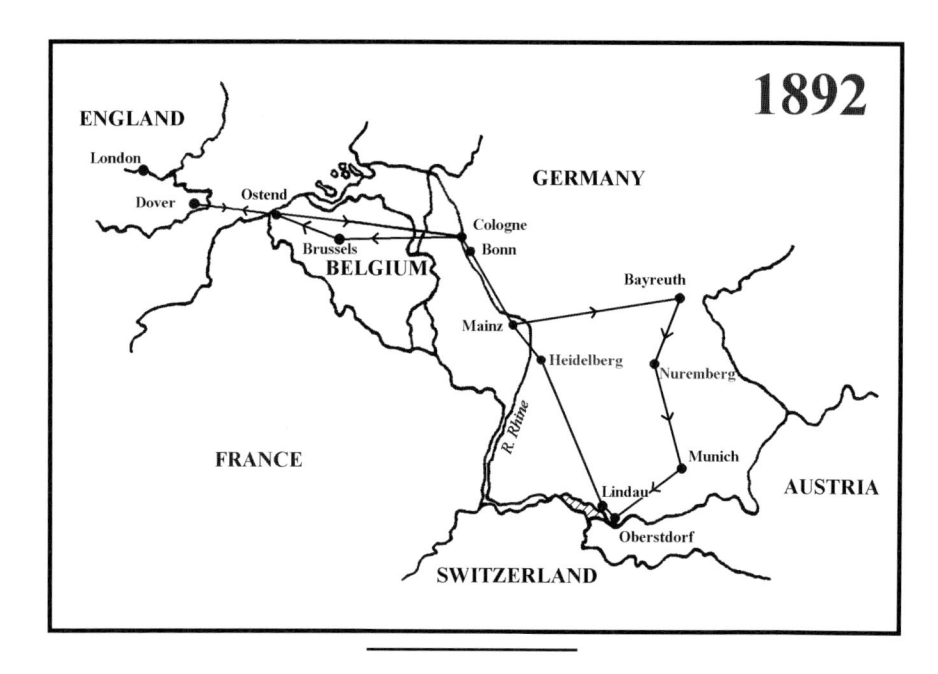

The next day, Thursday 28 July, having rested in the morning, the Elgars and Minnie lunched at the theatre restaurant at 4 o'clock before attending a performance of *Parsifal*. The following evening the party went to a performance of *Tristan*, and Alice noted the name of the opera in capitals in her diary.

Saturday 30 July was occupied by shopping expeditions but Alice's attention was occasionally diverted to observe some very fine butterflies and birds. On the Sunday it was Alice's turn to be unwell with a bad headache so she did not accompany Edward and Minnie to church, after which they went shopping again. Lunch at the theatre restaurant followed, by which time Alice was well enough to drive up to meet them and to accompany them to a performance of *Die Meistersingers*, beginning at 4 o'clock.

Parsifal was seen for a second time the next day. On this occasion, during the interval after Act I, Edward and Alice walked into the pine wood. But 1892 was the only visit to Bayreuth in the 1890s. During all the other holidays in this decade the Elgars saw Wagnerian opera in Munich. Bayreuth was not to be visited again until 1902, despite the fact

Journeys to and from Bavaria

that in those days *Parsifal* was not staged anywhere else.[3]

Nuremberg was the Elgars' next stop after Bayreuth. They arrived at 2 o'clock on Tuesday 2 August and found accommodation at Shlenk's Hotel, zum Goldener Adler. They drove round the walls in a "2 Gespann" (a type of horse-drawn carriage), then to the castle, to Albrecht Dürer's house, past the monument and fountains to Hans Sachs' house. Alice writes that they "caused mayhem". But how and why is not made explicit.

After breakfast the next day, they drove to the German museum and then walked back for lunch. Afterwards there was more church visiting, St Sebald's and St Laurence's. Edward posted a letter to his sister Pollie's children at Stoke Prior that he had penned the previous evening; it shows him to be deeply attached to his Grafton nephews and nieces :

Shlenks Hotel zum Goldener Adler
Nürnberg
August 2nd 1892

My dear May, Madge, Clare, Gerald & Vincent,

I thought I should like to send a line to you from this long way off, although I am afraid you will have to get your mother to read it, because this is a German pen & I cannot write well with it. Your Aunty Alice & I have come all this long way to here (*sic*) music at Bayreuth about which I will tell you all sometime & before we come back we hope to go a long way further to snowy mountains called the Algauer mountains. Now we are in Bavaria, they call it "Bayern" themselves & they are such nice, friendly people and so polite. If you go by a cabstand they do not say "Cab, please" but stand & bow & take their hats off and say "Ein steer" or "Zwei steer" which means one horse or two horses whichever they have. Most of the cabs have two horses & very fat & comfortable they look. Then the postmen who drive the mailcarts about the towns have white breeches, high top boots, bright blue coats & a brass horn slung round them & a shiny hat with a great white star in front: it is very hot here & the harness of all the horses is cover(*ed*) with loose fine pieces of leather like shoe laces & these wave about when they run & keep off the flies: some have gaudy silver & blue fringe(*s*) over their heads & a good many have foxes tails tied near their ears, to wag about also to keep off flies, & these do look funny. Then there are very few cart horses & the curious shaped wagons are drawn by oxen & they don't pull with collars like horses but have a bar across their foreheads & pull with their heads.

---

[3] Moore, Jerrold Northrop: *Edward Elgar - Letters of a Lifetime* (Oxford: Clarendon Press, 1990) pp 38-39

Then the guards of the train collect the tickets as the train is going along at full speed & he does not shout out "tickets please," but makes a bow & says "will the worshipful company be so friendly as to show their tickets!," & when he has seen them he says, "Thank you very much & good night, good travellers!," just think of that. There is not much coal burnt here but mostly wood: you don't buy it ready cut up but it's left in the street or yard & is in pieces about four feet long & then women come with saws & cut it up!

There is a very old castle within town & your mother will show you a poem by Longfellow[4] about the town which is one of the oldest in the country: & at the old castle there is a tower where they keep all the old instruments of torture, but we did not care to see them.

Then in all these towns there are every now & then fountains in the middle of the streets where the poor people fetch water from & most of them are very handsome & here especially, they are splendid looking & works of art. In Bavaria the national colours are blue & white & all the railway guards & porters are in bright blue which looks so pretty.

You would be surprised to hear the grasshoppers in the evening just as the sun is going down they make such a piping that it sounds like a tremendous noise; there are millions of them. Then there are large pine forests & it is so lovely to walk about in them. There are no hedges at all but like an open field as far as you can see.

Now I don't know if you can make this out but perhaps mother will. & with a kiss to you all and hoping you are having a nice holiday & much love to mother & your Daddy,

I am ever your affectionate Uncle.

Edward.

Your Aunty Alice is gone to bed but she sends her love to you all.[5]

On 4 August the party visited the Frauenkirche and then went on to Johannesbach. They saw the graves of Albrecht Dürer and Hans Sachs, and then the Rathaus before leaving for Munich at 4 pm. Nuremberg station is also described as "chaotic" and problems with luggage were encountered. Nevertheless they made a successful departure, arrived in Munich at 8.38 pm and went to stay at the Vier Jahreszeiten hotel.

One of the most interesting journeys on the 1892 holiday took place when they visited Lindau en route from Oberstdorf to Heidelberg. Their hotel presented them with a lovely view of the harbour. On 11

---

[4] 'Nuremberg', published in *The Belfry of Bruges and other poems* (1846) is a recollection of Longfellow's visit to the continent in 1842. It had been a favourite poem of Elgar's for a long time as he probably had shared his mother's enthusiasm for Longfellow.

[5] Moore, *op cit*, pp 38-39

Lindau harbour, visited by the Elgars in 1892
[Photo : J W Greaves]

August they boarded an Austrian boat to Constance across the lake. From there they took a train through the Black Forest to Heidelberg. Alice thought this journey very slow, tedious and uncomfortable. However, they eventually reached Heidelberg where they stayed at the Schloss Hotel overlooking the castle.

Years later, Elgar recalled this visit. He was sitting with Mrs Richard Powell (Dorabella of the *Enigma Variations*) on a bank overlooking the Severn River. He said that he "made her" (Minnie Baker) stamp and post the manuscript of *The Black Knight* when it was being sent to Novello. They posted it at Heidelberg, and Edward said he thought Minnie would bring him luck.[6]

It must have been lucky because later on in the year, on 11 November, he received a favourable reply from Novello. Yet it seems incredible that the whole of *The Black Knight* manuscript was taken by Elgar on holiday, and then, as he remembered, posted in its entirety at Heidelberg. Another Elgar scholar suggests otherwise when he states

---

[6] Powell, Mrs Richard: *Edward Elgar : Memories of a Variation* (Methuen & Co, 3rd ed 1942) p 2

that by 23 July the composer had completed enough of the vocal score to leave with Novello at their London office, as he and Alice passed through on their way to meet Miss Baker at Margate,[7] whilst the completed vocal and piano score was not posted to Novello until 30 September 1892.[8] So perhaps the manuscript posted at Heidelberg was just an instalment, for we are further informed that Edward did not begin the orchestral score until 31 December. The orchestration, duly completed, was posted to Novello on 26 January 1893.[9]

However, what is certain is that, on 12 August 1892 whilst at Heidelberg, Edward Elgar wrote a letter to his mother.[10] The letter contains a reminiscence of Henry Wadsworth Longfellow's semi-autobiographical prose romance *Hyperion*, which was a favourite book of Edward and his mother, and in which "A Beer Scandal" forms Chapter IV of Book II.[11]

---

[7] Moore, *op cit*, p 164

[8] *op cit*, p 166

[9] *op cit*, p 170

[10] Young, *op cit*, reprinted on pp 60-61

[11] Hyperion was also the book whence Elgar took the ballad poem which was to become his first large-scale choral work *The Black Knight*. He told the conductor Hans Richter in 1899 that it was the story "from which I, as a child received my idea of the great German nations." In it Hyperion, alias Paul Flemming (Longfellow's self portrait published in 1839) describes the poet's travels in Europe after the death of his first wife. One rainy afternoon in Interlaken, Paul picks up a volume of Uhland's poems and asks his companion, a beautiful English girl whom he desires, whether she has ever read anything by the German poet, and improvises for her benefit, a translation of *Die Schwarze Ritter*, a sinister medieval figure who rides into the lists during the feast of Pentecost and destroys the girl who dances with him and the young people who drink with him. Elgar however did not visit Tubingen where Uhland's birthplace is situated, at Neckerhalde 24.

Despite not being one of Germany's greatest poets, Ludwig Uhland (1787-1862) had had his verses set by Mendelssohn, Brahms and Schumann. In *Elgar* (Master Musicians Series, Dent, London, 1971) p 33, Ian Parrott suggests that the "horrific romanticism of his *Der Schwarz Ritter* appealed to the young Elgar, who, like many another enthusiastic young composer, did not wait to decide what impact any musical setting would have but simply used the lines to release his creative energy."

Heidelberg
August 12

Dearest Mother,

I must send a line from here about which we have read and thought so much. I have marked with a cross our hotel which is above the Castle. It is exquisitely lovely here and we are just going exploring. Last night we accomplished a good slice of the home journey - Lindau to Heidelberg - you will see on your map. Then when driving up here we suddenly had to stop and make way for a great procession of students - torchlight. The three duelling guilds with a brass band and marching - all their faces wounded (silly fools) & many with bandages on, gay uniforms & no end of torches: it did remind me of Hyperion & the beer scandal etc.etc.

I hope to send a few lines tonight if possible but trying to get everything in makes it so difficult to write: our tour seems to get more interesting as we proceed.

Dear A's eye is better & we are all well. I do miss not having a line from you but it was impossible to arrange where to stop. All we know now is Sunday in Cologne for the Cathedral Services.

I sent a line to Hubert (*Leicester*)

Much love to all
Immer and immer

Edward[12]

Earlier that day Edward had been out for a walk, again in the afternoon, and in the evening had seen the students' procession once more as well as lovely moonlight views of the Schloss and the Neckar.

1893

Following a rough crossing to Ostend, the Elgars again stayed at the Hotel du Nord in Cologne. This year they travelled from Cologne by river steamer to Bingen, and then on to Mainz by train. However, this holiday took them to Munich before going on to Garmisch. They returned to Munich, and stayed briefly at Cologne on the return journey.

---

[12] Moore, *op cit*, p 41

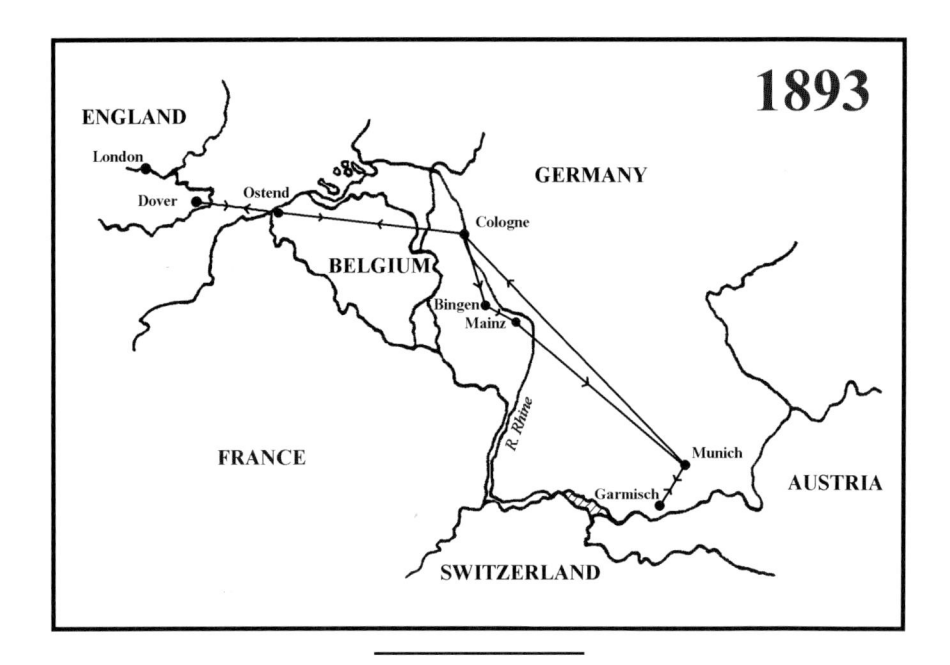

[Map: 1893 — showing England (London, Dover), Belgium (Ostend), Germany (Cologne, Bingen, Mainz, Munich), France, Switzerland, Austria, Garmisch, R. Rhine]

1894

The sea crossing in 1894 was from Harwich to the Hook of Holland, then Cologne again, and Munich. Their stay at Garmisch was interrupted by a brief visit on Thursday and Friday 16-17 August to Innsbruck, where they stayed at the Hotel d'Europe. Elgar was struck by his surroundings as Alice's diary shows:

> Much new snow on the mountains. Edward wildly rushing after engines. Lovely effect of the sun setting. Lights in snow and distant peaks.

Earlier that day, they made full use of their time as always by visiting the Schloss Ambras then, after lunch, visiting churches and walking about.

Their return journey featured Munich and Frankfurt where they only stayed overnight on Tuesday 18 September but still managed to visit Goethe's house. From Frankfurt, they travelled on to Bruges, which seems to have been a favourite place for the Elgars to visit, perhaps on account of its proximity to Ostend. They stayed there on 19 and 20 September when they visited the belfry and cathedral. In Alice's words they "heard unhappy chimes".

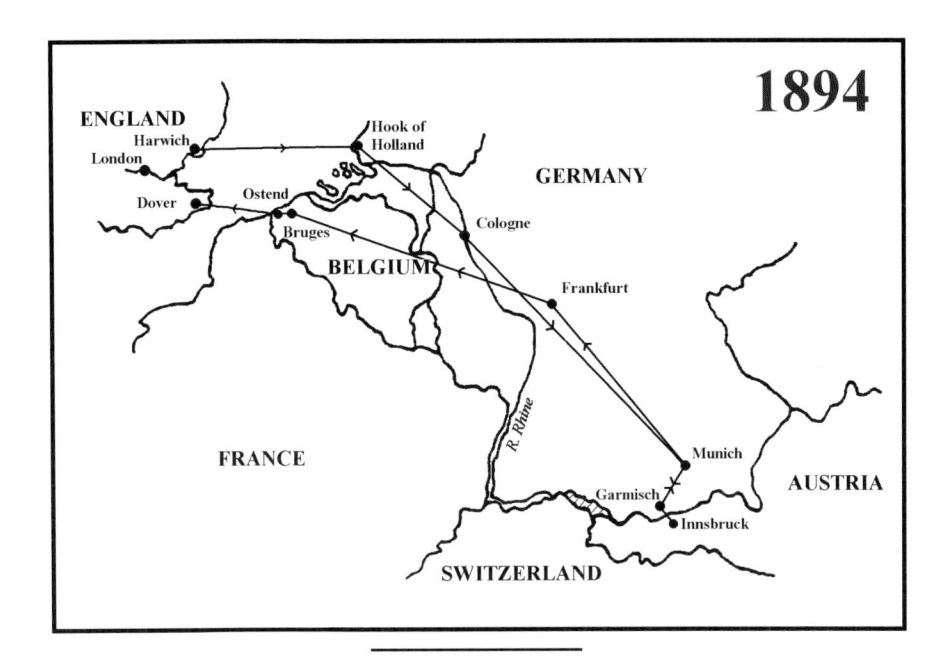

1895

Their journey to Garmisch this year was by a rather extended route and a somewhat hectic tour in which they were able to cram a great deal into a few days. On the outward journey they paid a return visit to Bruges from 31 July to 4 August, during which they visited several places of interest including the Beguinage, the cathedral (where they saw the Michaelangelo statue) and the Hospital St Jean to see the paintings by Memling. Unfortunately, on the Saturday Alice was poorly and spent most of the day in her room.

On Monday 5 August they arrived in Wurzburg. Alice's diary records that the city "was very fine and ...... all beflagged for a military fete". They visited the Residenz before leaving for Regensburg where they went into the cathedral. They later drove to Walhalla, the national monument modelled on the Parthenon. From Regensburg they boarded a boat at Passau on Thursday 8 August to sail down the Danube to Linz which, according to Alice's diary, was "very nice, only to (*sic*) cold and blowing".

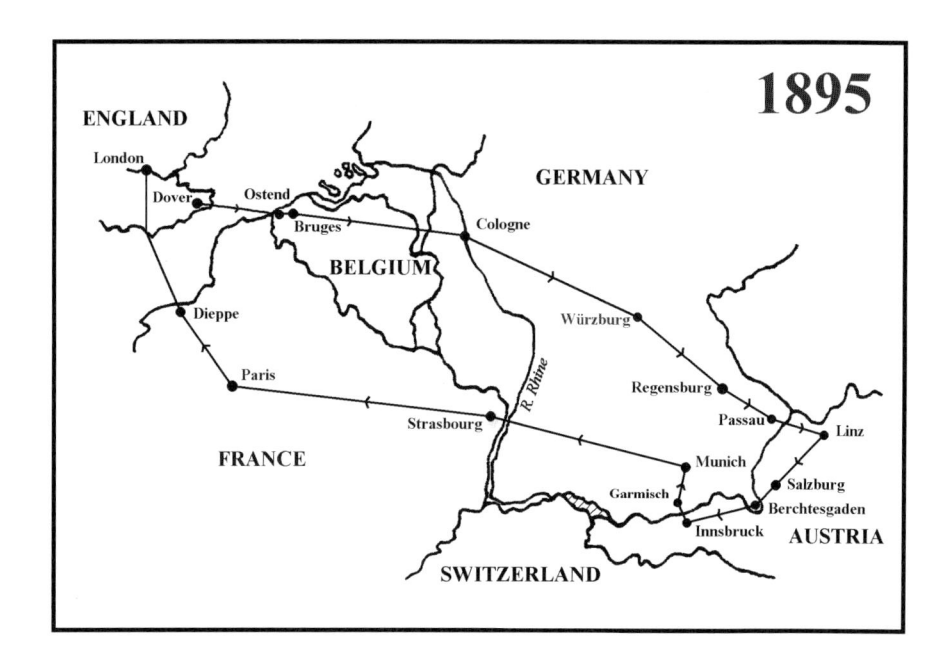

On 9 August they took a train to Salzburg where they stayed at the Hotel am Stein. The Elgars thought Salzburg "lovely", travelled on the cable railway and, on 10 August, visited Mozart's house. They then visited St Gilgen and St Wolfgang, both on the edge of the Wolfgangsee, on the 11th before arriving in Berchtesgaden the next day. Their room in the Hotel Vier Jahreszeiten was "horrid" and not to Alice's liking and they were none too satisfied with the alternative they were offered. Berchtesgaden was not a success. The weather was wet. They were damp and wretched after having been soaked to the skin in a thunderstorm. When they visited the salt mines at Bergwerkallee, Alice found having to dress in the miner's protective clothing "repellent".

There are inconsistencies between Alice Elgar's diary and Edward's notes over the next 10 - 11 days. From 15 to 17 August Alice's diary is blank. She states that she and Edward left for Innsbruck on Saturday 17th. Left from where? The last place mentioned in her diary was Berchtesgaden. If so, then it seems they spent some 5 - 6 days there, which is very unlikely given the unhappy diary records already mentioned.

Journeys to and from Bavaria

However, Edward's notes suggest that they spent 15-21 August at Kitzbühel. He mentions Tuesday 20 and Wednesday 21 August spent on Kitzbüheler Horn and places their departure from Kitzbühel for Kaprun and Mittenwald on 22 August. This is partially supported by a communication, fully descriptive of sights and sounds, sent jointly from Kaprun to Edward's mother on 22 August :

> 3.30 - we arrd here about ½ an hour ago: our "carriage" was like a large bath chair - a little horse harnessed with ropes. He bossed the whole show; took his own pace, chose his own road - stopped at every public house on the way & squealed at every horse he met - about four(.) It is lovely here: just at the entrance to our valley!
>
> Love, E.E.[13]
>
> We cd hardly believe the great mountain was not a cloud at 1st sight - our coachman aged about 15 - maintained it was a cloud! We hope to see something of the snow wonders at a safe distance(.) It has been such a lovely day, & we are so happy to be "out wild" - Trust you are all well with all love.
>
> Yr C.A.E.[14]
>
> All our luggage is at Innsbruck; we have our Rücksacks.

According to Alice Elgar's diary, having left for Innsbruck on 17 August, the following day they saw the Golden Roof built in 1500 by Maximilian I as a royal box, from whose balconies he and his guests could watch events taking place in the square below. Then they attended the Jakobskirke for Benediction. On Monday 19th, it was fearfully hot as they walked about Innsbruck before leaving for Garmisch by way of Seefeld, where they saw the church, and Mittenwald where they had lunch - a lovely day for a lovely drive. They arrived in Garmisch at about 5.30 pm and attended a fancy (dress) ball in the evening.

Of course the Elgars could have gone to Kaprun from Innsbruck but, judging from Alice's diary, there does not seem to have been time for this, especially when the long distance involved is considered. It is probable that Kitzbühel and Kaprun were visited en route, with their luggage having been sent on in advance to Innsbruck.

On their way home in 1895, the Elgars stayed in Strasbourg for two nights at the Hotel Terminus. Elgar was suffering from throat trouble

---

[13] *op cit*, p 48

[14] *ibid*

and had to consult a doctor who prescribed arrowroot. He was apparently well enough by 7 September to visit Strasbourg Cathedral. They continued their journey the following day when they arrived in Paris for a two-day stay at the Hotel des Deux Mondes. Most of their time was spent in the Louvre and Notre Dame Cathedral.

1897

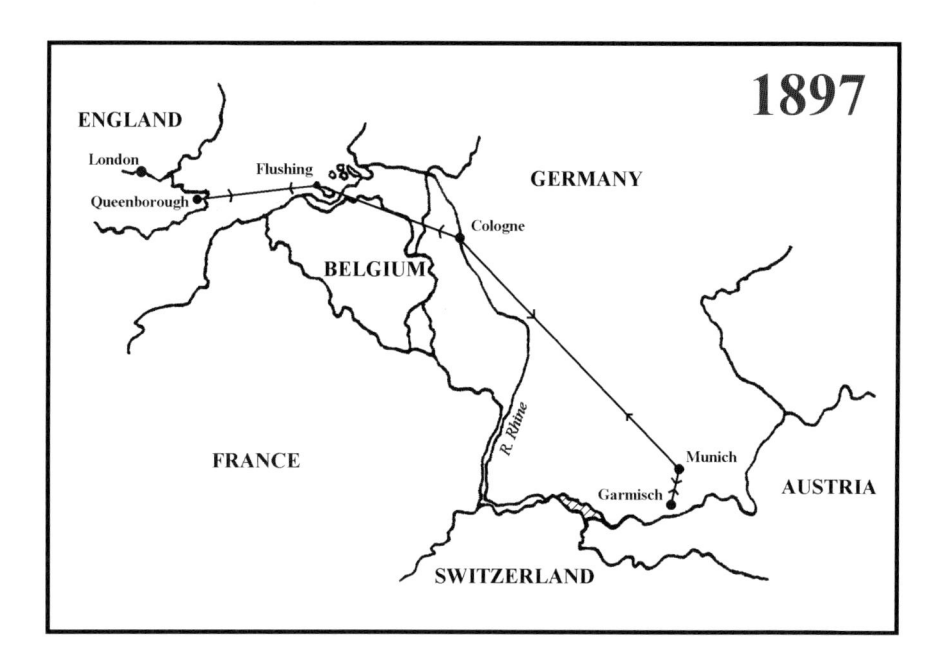

There was no Bavarian holiday in 1896, but in 1897 they crossed to Flushing and yet again travelled via Cologne and Munich before arriving at Garmisch. Again the return was by way of Cologne. As we have seen, the effective use of these journeys by the Elgars made them important parts of their German holidays.

Chapter Three

Munich

Undoubtedly the most significant venue visited by the Elgars on the way to and from Garmisch was Munich. Indeed, one of the main reasons for the Elgars' holidays in Bavaria was that on the outward or return journeys they could visit Munich where Edward could immerse himself in the music of Wagner. Although Elgar tended to discount the influence of Wagner in later-life remarks, at least two prominent scholars are in no doubt as to the importance of the Munich visits in affecting his development. According to one, they were "another lasting influence on his style".[1] Another felt that Elgar's regular trips abroad between 1892 and 1902 were in his formative "apprenticeship" years during which his "musical techniques and style were making their greatest consolidating advances".[2] On each of the five visits to Germany during this decade he saw productions of Wagnerian opera, many of them in Munich. There can be no doubt that Elgar's knowledge and understanding of Wagner "deepened most markedly" during this period.[3] Rosa Burley observed the early stages of this process at first hand when she tells us how Elgar was beginning to "understand very fully how the new music was put together" and how he could use this understanding in his own compositions.[4]

In 1892, when Minnie Baker organised the holiday, the Elgars travelled to Oberstdorf via Munich. They had arrived in Munich at 8.38 pm on Thursday 4 August and found the station chaotic. At first, a mislaid

---

[1] Parrott, Ian: *Elgar* (Dent, London, 1971) p 5

[2] Dennison, Peter: 'Elgar's Musical Apprenticeship' in *Elgar Studies* (Scolar Press, 1990) p 9

[3] *op cit*, p10

[4] Burley, Rosa and Carruthers, Frank C: *Edward Elgar - the record of a friendship* (Barrie and Jenkins, 1972) p 93

24 In The Bavarian Highlands

Above : the Central Railway Station, Munich around the turn of the century
Opposite : Alte Pinakothek (Old Picture Gallery), built 1826-36
Below : Konigliches Hof and National Theatre
[All photos : Schirmer/Mosel Verlag, Munich]

holdall caused luggage problems but eventually they checked in at their Hotel Vier Jahreszeiten. Unfortunately the next day Minnie was suffering from a slight cold and Alice had some sort of eye trouble. Nevertheless Alice was able to accompany Edward to the Alte Pinakothek (the Old Picture Gallery) after which Minnie, now apparently recovered, joined them for lunch at the Café Maximillian. Alice then consulted a Dr Aiche concerning her eye problem and frequent visits were paid during the rest of the day to the Apotheke S.Anna. There was, however, another short visit by Minnie and Alice to the Alte Pinakothek whilst Edward apparently took himself off on his own, and then in the evening went to a performance of *Cavalleria Rusticana*.

The 1893 visit to Munich was undertaken by Edward and Alice on their own without significant help from friends. When discussing the holiday with Rosa Burley, it was decided that the Vier Jahreszeiten would be too expensive.[5] Rosa advised Edward of her intention to "go into rooms" of which she had a number of addresses supplied by her German governess. If he chose to do so he could make use of the list. He and Alice did so and rooms were booked at 13 Gluckstrasse.[6]

---

[5] *op cit*, p 56

[6] *ibid*

The main purpose of the holiday was the Wagner Festival and, on the evening of their arrival in Munich on 17 August 1893, they - the Elgars, Rosa Burley and her pupil Alice Davey - all went to a performance of *Die Meistersinger* at what Rosa Burley calls the Vast Hoftheater. In earlier times the name of the theatre was Konigliches Hof und National-theater[7] but it exists today as the National Theatre, home of the Bavarian State Opera.

During their two-week stay they saw the following programme of Wagnerian opera:

Thursday 17 August	*Die Meistersinger* at 6 pm
Sunday 20 August	*Rheingold* at 7 pm
Monday 21 August	*Die Walkure* at 7 pm
Wednesday 23 August	*Siegfried* at 6 pm
Thursday 24 August	*Tannhäuser* parody
Friday 25 August	*Götterdämmerung* at 6 pm
Sunday 27 August	*Die Feen* at 7 pm
Tuesday 29 August	*Tristan* at 6 pm
Friday 1 September	*Tannhäuser* at 7 pm

This programme was mostly conducted by Hermann Levi, who was then approaching the end of his illustrious and long career as a conductor.

Rosa Burley tells us[8] that Elgar had an immense admiration for the part writing in the second act of *Die Meistersinger*, and in later years she was often reminded of that evening again; for there is, in the first movement of the Second Symphony, an unmistakable though doubtless unconscious reference to a well-known phrase in the opera. She was also later reminded of that evening, as Elgar chose the 'Wach Auf' chorus for the signature tune of the Worcestershire Philharmonic Society who sang it as a prelude to most of their meetings.

Rosa Burley was unimpressed by *The Ring*, chiefly on account of what she called "its interminable length" and she was quite unable to understand Elgar's enthusiasm for it.[9] *Tristan* was a shattering

---

[7] Correspondence (30 October 1996) from the Bavarian State Opera

[8] Burley and Carruthers, *op cit*, p 68

[9] *ibid*

experience and Alice was most affected by the "erotic music", even allowing for her somewhat superficial appreciation of King Mark's character - she called him "a thoroughly nice man". Yet all were emotionally affected by the music to the extent that "sleep was impossible for the whole night!"[10]

The opera performances had their lighter side and Elgar's amusement at the absurd aspects of operas was very great. Rosa mentions his schoolboyish sense of fun when "he was immensely tickled by the all-too-generous proportions of the Rhine maidens, and .... always hoped that the ropes which supported them would give way". The unathletic gods, with the terrible clubs with which they clumped on to the stage, also pleased him, as did the final moment when Levi tottered on to the stage, a small, stiff figure leading a vastly-proportioned Brünhilde to take her bow.[11]

On another occasion, on 24 August, Rosa, Alice Davey and Edward attended a parody of *Tannhäuser* at another theatre in Munich to provide an evening of light relief. "The humour - provided in the main by a Venus more huge than a Wagner soprano - was not very subtle and perhaps our imperfect knowledge of German saved us a certain amount of embarrassment, but we laughed so immoderately."[12] On this occasion Alice Elgar was not present.

For Elgar, Munich had other delights quite incidental to the music. Opera performances began in the late afternoon. During the Grosse Pause, Elgar's party retired to the theatre restaurant to restore themselves emotionally by drinking beer, accompanied by schnitzel, semmel brot and sauerkraut. There was probably a vigorous discussion of the performance up to that point.[13]

The real discussion, however, came after they had left the theatre and adjourned to the Hofbrauhaus. There the whole opera would be

---

[10] *op cit*, p 69

[11] *op cit*, p 70

[12] *ibid*

[13] *op cit*, p 69

reviewed, the playing criticised in detail and the technical means by which each effect had been achieved carefully analysed.[14]

Despite Edward's admiration of Wagner's music, he could still exercise his critical faculty. Rosa Burley recalls how he was unhappy with the coarse quality of the brass.[15] The stay in Munich was very much a working holiday for Elgar. He spent much time writing notes copiously on the performances and music he had seen and heard. Rosa's opinion was that Alice was responsible for exercising control because sometimes when they called to "take him out" she "would put her finger to her lips and tell us he was too busy".

> "My word," said Alice Davey (Rosa's pupil and companion), "doesn't she keep him at it?"[16]
>
> "She certainly did......"

Occasionally Rosa Burley felt that Alice kept him at it a little too much, though the result justified the means and Alice's methods. She felt that during a holiday in Munich expressly to enjoy themselves, Mrs Elgar's strictures were misplaced.

The background to Elgar's stay in Munich in 1893 relies heavily on Rosa Burley's account; apart from Alice's rather sparse and factual diary accounts mainly of events, Miss Burley's necessarily subjective views are all we have to fill in the details. Subjective they may be, but one is certainly left with the impression of a relaxed Elgar obviously intent on enjoying himself.

On the day after the Elgars' arrival in Munich in 1893 - Friday 18 August - they went to tea with Miss Burley and on this occasion she was struck by Edward's evident happiness at having found in Munich many new delights. These included the Biedermeyer furniture, the Munchener kind'l with beer mug, the ancient tea-caddy and its green-glass sugar box which Frau Würmer, the guest-house keeper, had produced to welcome her English visitors. Reference is also made to

---

[14] *ibid*

[15] *ibid*

[16] *ibid*

the origins of a family joke which occurred that afternoon and persisted for years. Whilst it seems a trivial matter in itself, it does give some indication of Elgar's state of mind. The German word 'Herrschaft' (usually meaning 'power' or 'reign') was brought into the conversation and Elgar, at the same time failing to appreciate its meaning and also taking it to refer to himself, commented "This Herrschaft is enjoying himself".[17]

Rosa Burley also gives an assessment of Alice's attitudes during the holiday. She seemed to be happy, though in a more restrained way than Edward. She was obviously very much at home with both the German way of life and Munich itself. She spoke excellent German and complimented Frau Würmer graciously on her tea and room arrangements. Rosa found Alice somewhat over-protective of Edward at times but perhaps these were the early signs and expressions of Alice's desire to further his career. Her attitude towards Edward was "that of the doting mother of a gifted son rather than a wife". She fussed over his health, sometimes to his irritation. Her "self-sacrificing" admiration for him was already apparent and she "seemed to feel that on every occasion she should act as general guide and mentor".

Rosa felt that Edward tried to live up to Alice's expectations and indeed succeeded in doing so, especially when, for example, he was explaining musical and operatic technical points. But on other occasions events conspired to embarrass them both. Sometimes, when he made an obvious mistake, it could be deflected as a joke. This applied to the often told story of the occasion when he took a horse tram intending to travel to the end of the route. He asked for the "letze Ruhe Platz" (literally the last resting place). He was put down at a cemetery. Edward told the story with great joy and amusement. And so it passed off.[18]

But on other occasions it seems as though he totally misjudged the situation and what might be Alice's reaction to it. Thus, when she expressed her admiration for Hans Sachs, Edward deeply offended Alice by suggesting "that a medieval shoemaker must have had coarse

---

[17] *op cit*, p 65

[18] *op cit*, pp 65-66

habits and had probably blown his nose between two fingers". Similarly when Alice expressed her enthusiasm for Brahms, Elgar commented, "Yes Chickie but don't forget that his favourite amusement in beer gardens was to take servant girls on his knee and tickle them". Not unnaturally, Alice's response to such indiscretions was to reply with irritation, "Really Eddu, I don't think we need dwell on that".[19]

It was a wonderful holiday in Munich in 1893. The Elgars saw all the sights of the city. For example, on 20 August they visited the Church of the Theatines with its bright-yellow rococo facade and twirly-topped towers - the church that contains the crypt mausoleum of the Wittelsbach family. The art galleries were especial favourites. The Alte Pinakothek was visited on 21 August, having been first seen the previous year on 5 August. When "Captain" Bethell came on Saturday 19 August 1893, the Neue Pinakothek captured their attention. Tuesday morning, 22 August, was spent walking. That evening the party, including Miss Burley and Miss Davey, went after dinner to a Lowënbrau Keller concert by tram.

Rosa Burley clearly remembers the visit to the National Museum on Thursday 24 August when she recalls Alice Elgar's emotion on looking at the blue and silver coronation robes of the unhappy young King Ludwig of Bavaria, who had befriended Wagner. A visit to the Nymphenberg Palace followed on 25 August. This they enjoyed immensely, set as it was in its acres of Versailles-style parkland and with its rococo decoration. However, their lunch at the Volksgarten was described as "horrid".

Several visits to various museums occupied their remaining days in Munich in 1893. The National again on Sunday 27 August, the Alte Pinakothek on 29 August and 1 September. This was also the day Edward bought the Wagner picture, a large engraved portrait which was to be hung in his study at home at Forli in a place of honour.

During this Munich visit Elgar was, according to Rosa Burley, unrecognisable because he expanded, laughed and enjoyed himself. The holiday had brought out the most charming side of Edward she had ever seen. In Malvern she had usually met him in circumstances

---

[19] *op cit*, pp 66-67

that seemed to make him feel ill at ease. He hated teaching and all the restraints of life in Malvern yet could not shake himself clear of them. But there in Munich he found a new freedom and an unaccustomed zest for life.[20]

Elgar clearly intended to enjoy everything that Munich could offer: the black beer, the sausages and the famous buildings. Rosa Burley describes the meals in restaurants and beer gardens. "We ate sausages in Hans Sachs. We had excellent suppers and heard music in the Biergartens, Hofbräukeller and Wiener Schnitzel in the Rathauskeller." They went about on little horse trams which ran till midnight. They went to Starnberger See with its lovely panorama of snow-covered mountains - the Bavarian Alps. They saw the lakeside villa in which King Ludwig had been living when he met his tragic death. Sometimes Elgar would say, "Oh think of Malvern" and they all sighed and groaned at the thought of going back to the stiffness and convention in that place.

Further visits to Munich took place in 1894 when they arrived on Thursday 2 August and stayed at the Hotel Belle Vue. Alice reports in her diary that Edward bought a straw hat and cloak. "He looks like a magician", she wrote. On their return from Garmisch on 13 September they stayed at the Hotel Bahnhof Garnie. The next day they saw Wagner's *Götterdämmerung* and, on Saturday 15 September, *Die Meistersinger*. Revisits to the Theatiner Kirche and the Alte Pinakothek were made. The Residenz was also visited.

In 1895, arriving from Garmisch at 1.30 pm on Wednesday 4 September, the Elgars attended *Der Fliegende Holländer* on the same evening, but thought it not well done. The next day Edward was "very badsley" and had to visit the chemist. They visited the Alte Pinakothek, but perhaps Edward's throat trouble was worsening as they left Munich the next day. So the 1895 visit does not seem to have been a particularly auspicious one.

The 1897 visit did not start too well either for, after travelling overnight from Cologne, they arrived in Munich at 8 am. Edward had such a "badsley headache" that Alice had to go to the opera to buy tickets on her own. However, by the evening Edward had recovered well enough

---

[20]　*op cit*, p 64

to attend a performance of *Tristan and Isolde* conducted by the 33-year-old Richard Strauss. He met Strauss after the performance. The Elgars left for Garmisch the next day but returned to Munich on Wednesday 1 September, and went to a performance of *Don Giovanni* at the Curvillies Residency Theatre. This was "lovely". Afterwards they again met Richard Strauss who had conducted the opera. The next evening the opera seen was *Der Fliegende Holländer* and on Friday 3 September the Elgars went to a concert in the evening before leaving Munich the next day for Cologne.

So concluded the intense experiences of Wagnerian opera during the visits of the 1890s. If, as has been suggested, for a self-taught composer the London concerts of the 1880s were his University, then Munich provided his post-graduate studies, informally perhaps, but with immense significance.

Marienplatz, Munich, in the 1890s
[Schirmer/Mosel Verlag, Munich]

Chapter Four

Oberstdorf

In 1892, Alice and Edward Elgar spent five days, from Saturday 6 August to Wednesday 10 August, at Oberstdorf in the Allgäu region of south western Bavaria. At 815m above sea level, this southernmost town in Germany is framed by the scenery of the Allgäuer High Alpine Chain wherein majestic mountains rise behind a market town which is surrounded by green meadows and woods. A dozen valleys emerge from the mountains like a fan, with Oberstdorf in its centre.

During this holiday they were accompanied by Mary Frances Baker, who had organised the holiday for them. The party had been staying for two days in Munich. From there they had travelled by railway train to Immenstadt,

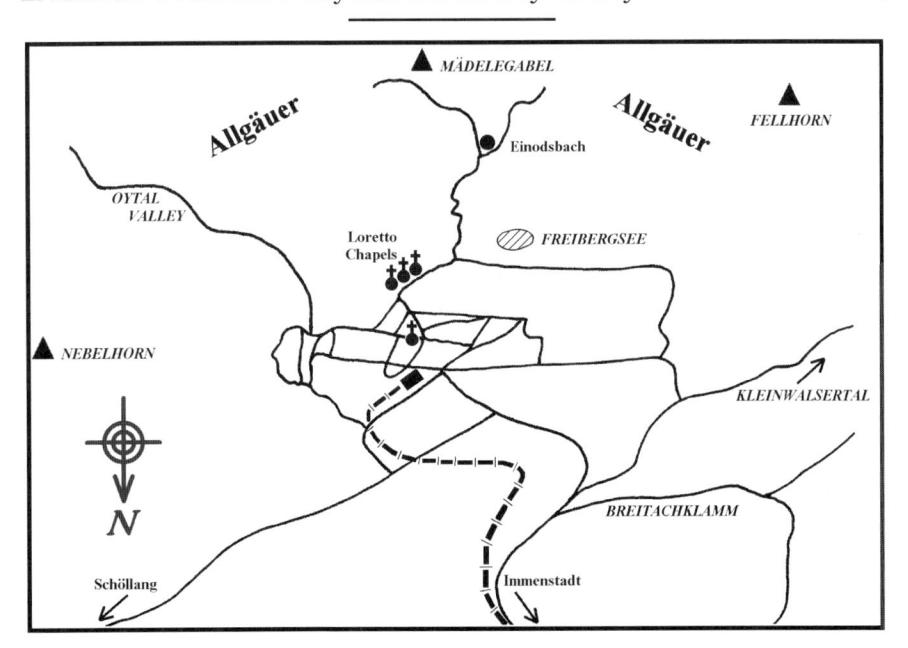

Oberstdorf 1892

a town to the north of Oberstdorf. The final part of the journey, on 6 August, was completed by road. As Alice wrote in her diary, "Drove off in a high old 2 Ge Span for Oberstdorf". They had obviously not booked accommodation because the diary states that the Mohren Inn had no vacant room. So they eventually found rooms at a saddler's.

On 8 August Elgar wrote to his nephews and nieces in the Grafton family:[1]

> My dear May and all of you,
>
> I wanted to send a line or two from this curious place and perhaps mother will read it to you if I write badly. We are now in a little village all among mountains upon which (some of them) high up in the clouds there is snow lying: & it looks very wonderful to see. Now all the houses in this little town are built of wood! & have balconies running round in which the people, in this hot weather have their meals & sit in the evening.

When the Elgars arrived in 1892 many of the buildings had been rebuilt quite recently. This was because, on 6 May 1865, a great fire had destroyed 146 buildings, amongst them the church, the school, the town hall and all the inns. Irreplaceable works of art and items of folkloristic value were lost. Then reconstruction began. The Rathaus (Town Hall) was rebuilt in 1888. A new road network was laid. Building styles changed and the parish church was re-built in a new Gothic style (page 37). And in 1888, just four years before Minnie Baker brought the Elgars to Oberstdorf, the tinkling bell of the small local train that ran from Immenstadt rang in a new age.[2] On a wall painting on Das Rathaus the little train, complete with smoke from the funnel, can be seen (page 37). The guard or porter is dressed in bright blue just as Edward had mentioned in his letter of 2 August from Nuremberg. Two mountaineers, or climbers, are to be seen arriving by train.

As Elgar wrote to his Grafton nieces and nephews:

> This is at the end of the railway - the mountains will not let it go any further and it is very strange to be here as no one speaks English & we are the only English people about anywhere.[3]

---

[1] Young, Percy M (ed): *Letters of Edward Elgar and other writings* (Bles, London, 1956), p 58

[2] Thoma, Eugen and Schlegel, Paul: *Oberstdorf,* Introduction

[3] Young, *op cit,* p 58

Panorama of Oberstdorf [J W Greaves]

Why did the Elgars come to Oberstdorf? Or rather why did Minnie Baker bring them to Oberstdorf? We know that, by 1892, tourism, especially hill-walking and mountain-climbing, had taken over from agriculture as the main source of the economy in the region.

Oberstdorf, however, was still, at that time, away from the mainstream of Bavarian tourism. It was a new resort - the railway had only just reached it. It had only five inns. A likely explanation lies in the fact that Minnie Baker, whose idea the holiday was and who organised it, may have heard about the town from her brother William Meath Baker, immortalised in the fourth of the Enigma Variations (W.M.B) and squire of Hasfield Court. He was very well known as a mountaineer. Indeed he was a member of the prestigious Alpine Club and had several first ascents in the Alps to his credit.[4] Probably he had climbed in the Oberstdorf area which, at that time, was attracting many hill walkers and mountain climbers as its first tourists. Could he have been climbing in the area at the time? Or did he recommend the area to Minnie, well anticipating the appeal it would have for Edward Elgar?

---

[4] *op cit*, p 339

Alice's diary records that on Sunday 7 August 1892, Edward and Minnie attended church at 9.30 am where Mass was celebrated to a setting by Kempter. The Elgars were certainly comfortable with the principal religious beliefs in this part of Bavaria. Elgar wrote to the Graftons:

> Now this is so different to England because it is a Catholic country & in this part there are no Protestants; & the church is open all day & you see workmen & workwomen carrying their rosaries & they go into the church as they pass by & say a few prayers (like you do without going to church) & then they come out of church & go on with their work, & then during mass at the elevation they ring one of the great bells in the church tower & all the people in the street know it is the elevation & take off their hats & make the sign of the Cross![5]

Hubert Leicester, who was then, in 1892, Choirmaster of St George's Church in Worcester, had asked Elgar to be on the look-out for German Catholic music which might be suitable for his Worcester choir. Elgar wrote to him:

> Now Bavaria being a Catholic country I have kept a sharp look-out for Church Music. At Oberstdorf, a little place in the mountains I heard a good Mass done by the villagers, very well conducted by the school-master with whom I subsequently became acquent (*sic*) : he let me look over their stock & I made notes thereon.
>
> I was sorry to find that the Mass I heard is only obtainable in separate parts i.e. organ pt, vocal pts & instrumental pts all separate - no score of any kind - so that would not be of any use: it was written by a man in Ausgburg & was very nice. In addition to the organ they had a Hautboy, Clarinet, Violin & a Trombone: the last made a ghastly noise.
>
> Now, I would not have bothered you with all this only to say amongst the other masses shown to me I have made a note of several which I think I should like: they are apparently, about the difficulty of F.Turner's mass, but more musicianly. No display & no flourishes, but plain, nicely harmonised music. Let me know if you care to hear more of them or if that sort of thing wd be of any use: I wd then enquire prices etc. which last I have not yet done as I thought I would tell you first what sort of things they were: send a line to Malvern or perhaps I shall see you.
>
> There was a requiem, but that was Gregorian, & the other things were much as usual: nowhere else I heard anything worthy of note: next Sunday we hope to be at Cologne on our way home but I expect there the music will be too elaborate to be useful. We have had a most delightful time: yesterday afternoon I was up in the eternal snow.....[6]

---

[5] *op cit*, p 58

[6] Moore, *op cit*, p 40

Oberstdorf 37

Left : The Rathaus, Oberstdorf, rebuilt in 1888 after a disastrous fire (p 34);
Right : Oberstdorf church (p 34)
[Both photos : J W Greaves]

Above : The three Loretto chapels (pp 39-40) - note that the drinking fountain, seen in the photo opposite, has since been removed;
Below : The tiny chapel at Einodsbach (p42)   [Both photos : J W Greaves]

Oberstdorf

The Loretto chapels, Oberstdorf, with the "common drinking fountain" sketched by Elgar visible in front of the nearest chapel. [Snell & Steiner]

After church on 7 August, Elgar and Minnie Baker walked from the church along the Prinzenstrasse. Here they experienced what Elgar describes again in his letter to his Grafton nieces and nephews:

> On the roads here there are crucifixes very often & generally a few trees planted round them for shade & people passing by stay & say a prayer & rest & then go on their way(s).
>
> Then on one of the roads here there are (one every 100 yards or so) the Stations of the Cross: doesn't that seem odd: & then at the end of them there are the three chapels to the blessed virgin.[7]

These are the three pilgrimage chapels of St Loretto surrounded by their centuries-old lime trees and situated on the road out of Oberstdorf to Birgsau and Einodsbach.

The first to be built, the small Appach Kapelle, was erected in 1493 at the instigation of Bishop Johann of Augsburg. The foundation stone of the Loretta Kapelle or Kapelle Maria Loretta was laid in 1657.

---

[7] Young, *op cit*, p 58

The interior of the second chapel contains an altar and altar piece with the Virgin and child standing behind a grill. It is a beautiful example of rococo gilded sculpture in which the figures of Mary and the baby Jesus are clothed in actual rich draperies.

The third Loretto chapel is the most recently built. It dates from 1671 and was called the Josef Kapelle. It was intended to mark the end of the way to the cross. In 1965 the interior of the Josef Kapelle was renovated; it remains in use for services. All three chapels contain valuable art treasures; as they were well away from the town, they fortunately escaped the effects of the great fire of 1865.

Elgar's letter to the Graftons mentions that "near the chapels there is a drinking fountain over which there is a monogram (mother will tell you what that is) - MARIA - that is not in the church but just a common drinking fountain by the roadside. How strange that would seem at Stoke. Like this....."[8]

Here, underneath the body of the letter, Elgar has drawn the monogram above the drinking fountain (see title page), copied from a sketch which he had made in his notebook, and which may be found at the Birthplace museum. Underneath he writes, "I daresay you can make it out. It is made of iron and gilt". The drinking fountain can be seen in the photograph on the previous page. Unfortunately, when the author visited the Loretto chapels at Oberstdorf, he discovered that the fountain is no longer there.

On this same Sunday, 7 August 1892, after pausing to look at the Loretto chapels, Edward and Minnie walked on through the woods to the Freibergsee. On their return, Edward went to see the schoolmaster to discuss musical matters and then they moved into a hotel, presumably the Mohren, "the things being carried up the street".

On the morning of the next day, Elgar and Minnie walked up the Oytal Valley, the entrance to which is across a bridge over a stream running down from the Seealpsee. The tree-lined path follows the bank of the stream. In summer the river runs over its rocky bed but it becomes a torrent in flood when the mountain snows melt in the spring.

---

[8]   *op cit*, p 59

Oberstdorf

Further along, the valley widens out (see picture on back cover) and is characterised at intervals by a series of lovely waterfalls. It seems likely, however, that Elgar and Minnie did not walk the whole length of the Oytal. There would not have been time because at 3.30 Edward again went to see the schoolmaster "and tried some music". Minnie and Alice drove to Schöllang, a village to the north of Oberstdorf.

Then Edward walked to Zwingsteg over the Austrian border to the Walserschanzle. Until 1900, and thus during the Elgars' time here, Zwing was the name given to an amazing gorge which is now called the Breitachklamm. This is a deep, impressively curling, riverine gorge, very narrow in places, with the gushing white waters of the Breitach river shooting over mossy rocks, and lined by ancient forests. It was allegedly haunted by spectres called Zwinggeister. The gorge gave its name to the nearby hamlet of Zwingsteg.

On the next morning, 9 August, the Elgar party went further into the Kleinwalsertal. They "started at 9 (in a 2 span) for Mittleberg *(sic)*", some 13.5 kilometres from Oberstdorf. It was a dull, cloudy morning but nevertheless they got out of the carriage and then walked to Zwingsteg and on to the Walserschanzle in Austria. Lying south-west of Oberstdorf, the Kleinwalsertal is indeed an enclave of Austria which, because of the mountains, can only be reached from Germany and has typical wooden farmhouses within a dramatic Alpine setting.

It is often believed that this Oberstdorf holiday was spent on the Austrian border but this statement needs clarification based upon a detailed knowledge of the area. The Kleinwalsertal - literally small Walser valley - is something of an oddity. In the 13th century the Walser-German emigrants from the Upper Valais (now in Switzerland) populated this previously uninhabited valley of the Breitach river. Through the centuries the Walsers, although technically in Austria, felt cut off from the rest of Austria by the Allgäu Alps. Then in 1891, the year before the Elgars arrived, this isolated valley was granted special status in which the police were Austrian, acting under Austrian law, whilst there were German customs officers, a German postal service which operated with Austrian stamps, and the only legal tender was the Deutschmark and not the Schilling.

By the late morning at the Walserschanzle it was pouring with rain. So the Elgar party drove back from there to Oberstdorf for lunch. Afterwards it was a lovely afternoon so they started to drive to Birgsau. Here they got out and walked up towards Einodsbach along the Stillach valley. Elgar's letter to the Graftons gave a graphic account of what such walks might be like:

> When you walk here up the valleys between these mountains a great many lizards come running about, very pretty to see but rather startling: some are no longer than my hand but some are quite long & run: then there are millions of butterflies: sometimes so thick that they seem like a cloud when you are in them: & then there are more & larger grasshoppers than ever half as long as my finger & bright green & they jump yards & make such a noise.[9]

Elgar was apparently also troubled by flies:

> I forgot to tell you of the flies here - not house flies - but out of doors they sting very much & draw blood, they fix themselves on your hands & before you know they have stung you like sticking in a pin & a little spot of blood comes & your uncle Ted does say some curious things.[10]

Eventually the walk took them to Einodsbach, with its tiny chapel cum shrine (pictured on page 38), and high up there at 1142 metres, in the southernmost village in Germany, "Elgar and Minnie walked on to the lavine and touched snow".[11]

The next morning, 10 August, the Elgars and Minnie Baker were seen off by the saddler's wife who had brought flowers for them. They left Oberstdorf by train at 11 am for Immenstadt and from there caught a connecting link to Lindau. It had been "an enchanting week". Elgar had spent a great deal of time noting the local folklore, and showing great interest in the ecclesiastical architecture and wayside shrines. Once Minnie Baker had introduced her friends, the Elgars, to Munich and Bavaria there was obviously the intense desire to go again to enjoy more Wagner, Munich and mountains!

---

[9] *op cit*, pp 59-60

[10] *ibid*

[11] Alice Elgar's diary quoted in Moore, Jerrold Northrop: *Edward Elgar - A Creative Life* (Oxford University Press, 1984) p 164. Here Alice probably intended to use the German word "Lawine", meaning an avalanche or snowfall. Its use here refers to the snow-line of the Berge de Guten Hoffnung (The Mountains of Good Hope).

Chapter Five

Garmisch

The *Bavarian Highlands* music, in its various forms - choral-orchestral, choral-piano or the *Three Bavarian Dances* - arose out of the holidays the Elgars spent in the lovely Garmisch-Partenkirchen area or Werdenfelser Lands in 1893 and 1894. They were to enjoy further holidays there in 1895 and 1897.

Alice's poems, together with Edward's musical accompaniments, were centred on this area and at that time Garmisch and Partenkirchen were two adjoining villages, but separated by open country. Indeed, Partenkirchen was the larger, more important town, more so as a trading and shopping centre than Garmisch, which remained of a rural nature with a mainly agricultural economy. At the time of the Elgars' visit, it was merely a village. Tourism based on walking and mountain climbing was

Garmisch, seen from the west in 1900 [Martin Schöll]

Garmisch's old railway station, seen here from the north   *[Martin Schöll]*

in its infancy. But, with its growth based upon winter sports and assisted by the construction of the railway link to the area in 1889, Garmisch gradually achieved equal status until, in 1935, in preparation for the 1936 Olympic Winter Games, the two adjoining villages were fused together into the one market town of Garmisch - Partenkirchen by order of the central German government. Fortunately, there was little if any damage to Garmisch during the two World Wars since the Elgars' visits.

The centre of the village (as local people still refer to it) of Garmisch is now the Marienplatz. It is much changed from the market place as it was referred to in Elgar's time in the 1890s, although many buildings from that time still remain. The Alte Apotheke, the town's oldest pharmacy, lends the Marienplatz a particular charm, as it did the old market place. Built in 1792, it stands on the site where the former blacksmith's shop stood. The same applies to Clausings Posthotel next to it. In 1620 it was "Die Alte Gasthaus zur Traube" and the proprietors held the sole rights for the import of wine from Italy.

One outstanding landmark, rising above the other buildings, is the so-called "new" Catholic Parish Church of St Martin (page 55). Built by

Marienplatz, Garmisch, in 1886 [*Martin Schöll*]

Josef Schmutzer in 1730-34, it is clearly the work of a master and a splendid example of rococo architecture. Here the Elgars would have attended Mass regularly although once, on Sunday 1 September 1895, they went to the "old church". This, with its pointed spire, is situated in the older part of Garmisch. It is basically a Romanesque church and has "walls studded with a biblical picture book from the Gothic period and a gigantic, Romanesque Christopherous".[1] Close by here is one of the oldest hostelries in the Bavarian Alps, the Husar, with its unusual façade painting: from a blind window two soldiers, one a hussar, look down on to the street below.

Returning to St Martins, close by, on a little grassed area, stands the Polz'n Kaschper's Haus (page 55), an irreplaceable example of the oldest type of house of this area and preserved almost unchanged for some 300 years. This house stands in the Möhrenplatz and it would certainly have been there at the time when the Elgars took their

---

[1] Adam Colour Guide: *Garmisch - Partenkirchen*. In the Alte Kirche, a large number of 15th and 16th century murals have been uncovered, especially the huge representation of St Christopher.

Die Drei Mohren inn, Garmisch, seen above in 1930 and, below, with convivial patrons in 1909 [Both photos : Martin Schöll]

Garmisch

holidays. The Möhrenplatz is so named because in this square stood Der Drei Mohren inn. This inn, however, no longer exists, having been demolished in 1980; although photographs do exist of what the inn was like in earlier times, and also of the convivial group of patrons in Bavarian costume assembled outside the hotel entrance.

It was at this inn that Edward Elgar saw the Bavarian Schuhplättler dancers. When Rosa Burley and some other authors called them Tyrolean, they were quite wrong. The Tyrol, we are strongly reminded by our Bavarian friends, is a quite different area lying to the south of the Garmisch region. Rosa does, however, give us an accurate account of what took place during the dancing, also vividly portrayed in the Herkomer painting "Schühplattler" dating from 1875 and reproduced on the front cover.[2] She describes how, in the large dining room of Der Drei Mohren, the dancers performed the Schühplattler to the zither music which inspired Elgar's songs *From the Bavarian Highlands*. The dancing, involving vigorous hand-clapping over and under the legs, had a gaiety which she always recalled every time she heard Edward's Bavarian music. Rosa is at pains to emphasise the originality of Elgar's tunes; they were not merely copies of those heard at the inn but they did recall for her the spirit of the dances and their music.[3]

Some characteristics of the houses in the village of Garmisch were of great interest to Elgar. The Sonnenstrasse (page 56), with St Martin's Catholic Parish Church seen in the distance, shows the wooden balconies in which he was particularly interested. In his note book at the Broadheath Birthplace Museum there are sketches of carved wooden balconies which fronted the houses.

He was also interested in, and sketched, the long water spouts which then projected some 6 to 8 feet in order to carry rainwater well away from the houses. Today, some of these older buildings are still in existence with their wooden balconies and piles of chopped wood, ready for the winter.

---

[2] See *Sir Hubert von Herkomer - a Catalogue of the Centenary exhibition celebrating his Mutterturm in Landsberg* (1988) p 28

[3] Burley, Rosa and Carruthers, Frank C: *Edward Elgar - The Record of a Friendship* (Barrie and Jenkins, 1972) p 70

As Elgar noted in his diary/book:

> Old men in the village with an immense heap of fir wood and trimmings, making two heaps, one of wood and the other of green shoots.

Some way east of the Marienplatz, just off the Bahnhof Strasse, is Dr Richard Strauss Platz in the pedestrianised Am Kurpark. Here is also the Richard Strauss Congress Centre, which is a reminder that in due course Garmisch became celebrated because Richard Strauss lived here for the greater part of his life (1908-1945). He lived in a fine house and garden with his initials appropriately incorporated into his garden gate. Richard Strauss's tribute to Elgar after the second German performance of *Gerontius* at Düsseldorf in 1902 should be remembered at this point : "I raise my glass to the welfare and success of the first English progressivist, Meister Edward Elgar." When we hear Richard Strauss's *Alpine Symphony*, we remember that the inspiration for this Bavarian music was the Zugspitze, at 2963m the highest peak of the Bavarian Alps, below which Garmisch lies. In this work, we wander in a mountain world in all its moods, from sunrise to sunset, a sound picture of this beautiful but awe-inspiring region.

Garmisch lies just to the north of the long Wetterstein mountain range with several mountainous peaks, from the Dreitorspitze (2633m) in the south east through the Alpspitze (2620m) to the precipitous Waxensteine and Zugspitze in the east. The Elgars would certainly have walked near the Zugspitze but there is no evidence that they climbed even part of the way up it. Edward admired the towering mountain, however, and was inspired to write about it in his notebook:

> - the summit of the Zugspitz .... is occasionally visited by "An Eagle" that is to say a particular one - although his special markings are not given -; those being fortunate enough to meet with this eagle on the top of the mountain may, on certain conditions, obtain from him a key. This is the key of the island in the Bader See, (a small green lake about three miles from G) thus equipped, the possessor of the magic key may unlock the island & secure to himself the treasures of the earth which are concealed there & he may presumably live happily ever after.
>
> This exploit, curiously enough, seems never to have fired the Bavarians; possibly because in this delightful land much wealth does not seem necessary to give great happiness: apparently this last consists chiefly in a sufficiency of Munich beer: the sufficiency varying with the individual, but at the lowest computation may be fixed at many litres per diem.

Garmisch

By the time the Elgars arrived in Garmisch there is evidence of the existence of quite a sizeable English community. There were the Slingsby-Bethells, with whom the Elgars stayed, and who arrived to settle in Garmisch in 1888-89. The so-called "English Colony" with its Anglican chapel (which was vandalised during the 1939-45 war and finally demolished in 1957) had a married couple and their family, the Foster-Wards, as its founders in 1880. Foster-Ward was a retired Colonel who had four daughters, Mary, Undine, Eda and Gertraud. According to the diary of one Garmisch resident, Emma Bodenmuller, another Englishman arrived in Partenkirchen in 1880. He was a Mr Egerton who rose from comparative poverty to become Lord Wilton as a result of the deaths of his father and elder brother. He eventually owned the Villa Victoria where many distinguished guests stayed, even the Countess of Teck with her daughter, Mary, who was to become the Queen of England.

The Elgars were met at the station on Saturday 5 August 1893, and the next year on Friday 3 August, by at least one of the Slingsby-Bethell children: Eustace in 1893, John in 1894, and possibly Mary in 1897. They would then be escorted to the Villa Bader.

During their holiday in Garmisch the Elgars would walk, equipped with rucksacks, to places over typical Bavarian scenery, in which the lowland would merge into the lower tree-lined slopes of the hills and mountains. One or two of the places and areas indicated in the subtitles to the songs in *From the Bavarian Highlands* choral suite were favourites, such as the St Anton chapel in Partenkirchen, and Hammersbach. On the other hand some of the sub-titled places are not mentioned in Alice's diaries.

Nevertheless, all the time Edward and Alice were absorbing the atmosphere, watching the dancing and listening to the songs of the Bavarians. They gathered a harvest of impressions:

> Swallows feeding young in houses, flying in and out over doorways left open for their pretty sight.......
> Rain - thunder - retired to cottage - peasants played and sang in parts, fresh from the hay cutting etc. Shook hands all round. Walls of room covered with horns......
> Haymakers remain on hills all night - fires lighted up in evening - cows coming home - bells, light wagons drawn by oxen.[4]

---

[4]   Quoted in Moore, Jerrold Northrop: *Edward Elgar - A Creative Life* (Oxford University Press,1984) p 175

All experiences which were to lead up to and influence the composition of the *Bavarian Highlands* music, if not directly then certainly subconsciously.

What do we know of the places sub-titled in the choral suite, *From the Bavarian Highlands*? One such place was Sonnenbichl, a little way to the north of Garmisch. Elgar himself wrote, in a letter of December 1900, that Sonnenbichl was a wooden gasthaus in the mountains and a favourite beer resort of his. Sonnenbichl today is far less romantic, being rather built up with a large hotel and housing developments, but still sunny! An early print dating from 1835 would seem to confirm Elgar's description; however a photograph taken in 1890 possibly suggests that the phrase "in the mountains" is slightly exaggerated. There is certainly a background of mountains when Sonnenbichl is viewed from Garmisch. Alice's diary does not record any walks to Sonnenbichl although an expedition in that direction, to Maximilian's höhe and the Kramerplateau, is mentioned as taking place on Wednesday 6 August 1893.

Wamberg is a village up in the hills on the western side of Garmisch. The village church may just be glimpsed from a lay-by on the road from Garmisch to Mittenwald. It is an hour's walk from Partenkirchen and, at 996 metres, is the highest village in Germany; as such, it is still a small, rather isolated village which can only be reached by hilly footpaths.

As the Elgars moved out into the country they would walk through Hammersbach to Grainau, both villages lying to the south east of Garmisch. On one such visit to Hammersbach, tea was brewed in a coffee pot for there were no teapots in the whole of Hammersbach. It was served to them as a "black concoction" and the daughter of the house, in honour of the visitors, felt obliged to put on stockings though not shoes! As a storm broke when they were in the cottage, the Elgars stayed to shelter and were thrilled when, as the men came home from the fields, the little community spontaneously broke into four part harmony.

Hammersbach lies at the foot of the Höllenthal (now Höllental). This rugged mountain gorge (1047-1193m) is awe inspiring. It is approximately one kilometre long and was originally accessible, in the Elgars' time, from the front side. A bridge, 29 metres long and 73 metres high, was built in 1888 over the Hammersbach river to gain access to the upper path.

Garmisch

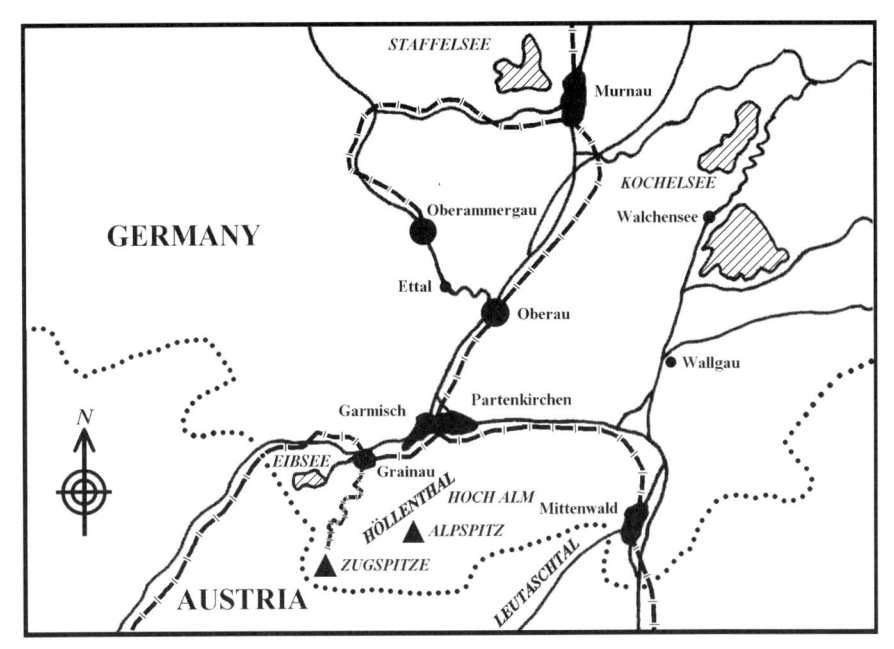

The Elgars' visits to the Garmisch area

According to Alice's diary, an expedition to the Höllenthal took place on Friday 11 August 1893, and the visit was repeated on Tuesday 17 August 1897 when they were accompanied by the Prendergasts and "Captain" Bethell; they enjoyed a "most lovely" time. Both Mr H D Prendergast, a close friend from Garmisch, and Mr Bethell were to subscribe to the purchase of Elgar's Cambridge doctorate robes in 1900.

During their holidays, the Elgars visited the pilgrimage chapel of St Anton (Sankt Anton - page 56) three times: on 9 August 1893, 11 August 1894 and again on 24 August 1897. On the 1894 visit, the Elgars were accompanied by the Fittons - Mrs Fitton and her daughters Isobel and Hilda (close friends from Fairlea in Graham Road, Malvern) - who were touring Germany that summer and who had come to spend four days with the Elgars in Garmisch. The chapel stands on the lower slopes of the Wank mountain, forty metres above Partenkirchen, and is accessible by a footpath. It was originally constructed as a chapel in 1708 as a gesture of gratitude for the sparing of Partenkirchen village during the War of the Spanish Succession. The chapel was enlarged between 1734-

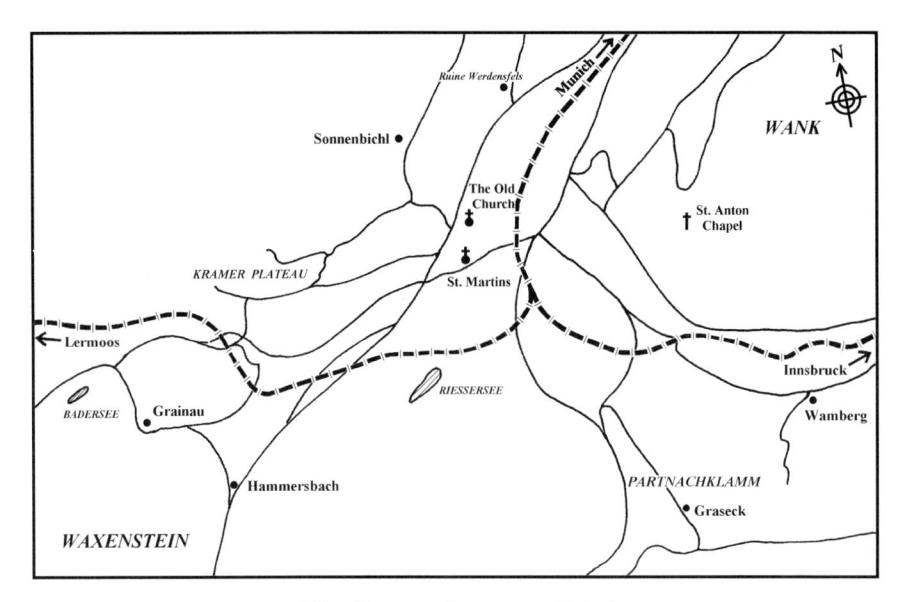

The Garmisch area in detail

1736 by Joseph Schmutzer and the ceiling frescos were designed by Johann E Holzer. On the walls of the corridor leading up to the chapel entrance is a moving reminder of the human costs of war: the walls are covered with picture plaques of soldiers killed in more recent conflicts.

Seen from the outside, the two parts of the building look like rather plain squares but, inside the chapel, the parts merge with considerable charm, architecturally speaking. Two aisles are formed, both covered by dome-shaped ceilings. Indeed, the Holzer ceiling painted in 1739 is a most striking feature. Other painted scenes in the chapel are also thanksgivings for the three occasions the town and chapel were delivered from destruction in war.

It was from Partenkirchen that Elgar sent a postcard to Carice, his daughter, expressing greetings on her third birthday. It reads "Best birthday wishes from father and mother. Here is a nice little chamois and a Bavarian man, Love E.E." This postcard, now in the Birthplace Museum collection, was reproduced on the record sleeve of the first recording of the orchestral version of *From the Bavarian Highlands* by

Photograph of Elgar taken in Partenkirchen during their 1897 holiday by local photographer B Johannes and subsequently published in the March 1898 issue of The Minim *magazine [The Elgar Birthplace Museum]*

the Bournemouth Symphony Chorus and Sinfonietta. Recently it has been reproduced in *Dear Carice: Postcards from Edward Elgar to his Daughter* [Osborne Books Ltd], a collection from the archives of the Elgar Birthplace Museum.

Visits to Partenkirchen, in addition to the St Anton pilgrimages, were made on 8 and 9 August 1893 when they "saw the Prince Regent..... Splendid uniforms to be seen." It was also on the occasion of a later visit, on 26 August 1894, that Edward bought Alice a cowbell bracelet. She thought it "quite lovely".

When they visited Partenkirchen on 2 September 1895, Alice and Edward were photographed by B Johannes. Edward was photographed by the same person on 14 August 1897 and the head and shoulders of the print was published on page 144 of *The Minim* in

March 1898.[5]   Their final visit to Partenkirchen took place on 22 August 1897, making a total of five visits, plus the three to St Anton.

The fifth song of *From the Bavarian Highlands* is sub-titled 'On the Alm (Hoch Alp)'. Unfortunately there is no record of Alice and Edward ever having walked there, at least not in Alice's diary. The Hoch Alp is a mountain pasture to the south of Hammersbach. Here in summer a peasant girl, often called a Hüterin or Sennerin, would live in a hut to tend the grazing cattle. Writing in his diary-cum-notebook, once described as a "sketchy performance not a strict one," Edward tells of the cows with their bells coming home. Years later the sound of the cowbells heard in this countryside was to appear in Elgar's score for *The Starlight Express*. Today Hoch Alm may be visited by taking two cable cars - the Alpspitzebahn and the Hoch Alp Grosse Bahn.

The sixth song 'The Marksman' (Bei Murnau) is set against the background of the Staffelsee. This is now a popular bathing lake and the town of Murnau is situated nearby. One visit was paid here on 11 September 1894. There were expeditions to places other than those mentioned in the sub-titles of *From the Bavarian Highlands*. The most popular seems to have been to the Riessersee and the nearby Riesserbauen which was visited six times: on 10 August 1893; 8, 11 and 23 August 1894; 10 September 1894; and, finally, on 16 August 1897. This southern side of the Garmisch valley is particularly picturesque. The Riessersee entails quite a short walk and on Thursday 23 August 1894, it was sufficiently near for an evening visit after a very hot day. "Edward rowed Alice about on the lake."

Other lakes in the district had their attractions. The Elgars would walk to the Badersee and Eibsee, occasionally accompanied by Henry Slingsby-Bethell who was with them on Monday 7 August 1893. In 1894 when the weather became hot, "too hot to do anything" according to Alice, they nevertheless walked to the Eibsee on Tuesday 22 August by way of the Badersee. They rowed on the Eibsee, lunched in the woods and walked all the way back, arriving at the Villa Bader at 6.15 pm. Today the Eibsee is a popular all-year-round venue. It is an idyllic alpine lake which nestles against the backdrop of the magnificent mountain range rising straight up to a height of 2000 metres. In the

---

[5]   Copy at Elgar Birthplace Museum, Broadheath

Garmisch

The Catholic Parish church of St Martin, Garmisch, seen (left) from the Marienplatz and (right) with Polz'n Kaschper's Haus (p45) in the foreground [*Both photos :J W Greaves*]

56 In The Bavarian Highlands

Left : The Sonnenstrasse, a typical Garmisch street showing the wooden balconies which Elgar sketched (p 47). The tower of St Martin's church can be seen in the distance;
Right : The St Anton chapel today (see p 51)
[Both photos : J W Greaves]

Garmisch

Elgars' time the natural setting was virtually undisturbed, the first hotel not being built until 1913.

Then there were expeditions further afield. In both 1893 and 1894 the Elgars visited Oberammergau, famous for its passion play and theatre, and only a short distance from Garmisch. On the earlier visit, on Sunday 13 August 1893, Alice records in her diary:

> Mass at 9.20 then to Oberammergau all day in a Stellwagen with the Archbishop, Mr Bethell, Phillip and Lennon/Lennard, Mrs Young, Miss Penney. Disappointing and expensive, enjoyed wood carving and paying a visit to the theatre. In the evening saw village play "Du Blume von Sicilien." Back about 7.30.

In the following account in his diary, Edward suggests that the visit might have taken place on Tuesday 15 August:

> Looking into my diary.... I see under date Monday August -, 189-, Sat out long in evening talking with R - a farewell, he [is] leaving for Munich next morning......
>
> R said "The Archbishop is to arrive tonight: I am sorry I am going, somewhat on that account, for there is no end of excit.ement in the house." I assented; there had been indeed a great deal of talking in various languages during the last few days - "the Archbishop of N - would honour the "Villa B" with his presence for some time; he would come by Stellwagen from Innsbruck," - "he would say mass every day in the large church," - " & he was to arrive on the - th' -" that was tonight.
>
> In the drawing room, whither I retired, nothing much was doing: a few going to Ober-Ammergau in the morning were putting finishing touches to their plans; a play was to be performed by the villagers & a Stellwagen was engaged to drive us over. A & I agreed to go & when I had played through half an act of Tristan, including Kurvenal's "Spott-lied", sung in stentorian tones by Herr B, - someone began to read aloud "Die Blume Von Sicilien" - the Ober-Ammergau play of the morrow.
>
> In the midst of this a rattling of wheels was heard & some barking of dogs. Various sounds of confusion added to these drew us to the balcony &, looking out, we saw lights waving & a small crowd of villagers and the Catholic inhabitants of the house gathered round a carriage with smoking horses. The driver swung himself from his perch holding the brake with one hand & the near horse's tail with the other & running to the door, allowed a portly fine looking old gentleman (to) alight - the villagers & the guests knelt & kissed the old gentleman's hand as he passed by - it was the Archbishop.
>
> I retired to find R & report. He was in the kitchen (that being the only room having a fire) busily employed in making holes in a strap preparatory to the morning journey: this accomplished with a red hot gimlet, - an evil smelling performance in which Hieronimo (the Italian cook.....) was much interested. I told R of the joy of the Archbishop's arrival & how he had promised at once to join us in our Ober-Ammergau expedition. "Then I will stay another day," said R. But "if I go to Oberammergau it will be as a pilgrim." We had reason to remember these words ....

Hieronimo knew the Archbishop who, it seems, was to enter so largely in our lives: he had seen him - and cooked for him - in Rome - "How is he for a man," I asked, Hieronimo strummed softly on the guitar & mused - "He is a good man," he said at length - "he takes much oil in his salad."[6]

On entering Oberammergau, one passes down the main street with its typical Bavarian houses and their balconies. Then, in a turning off to the left is a road leading to the passion play theatre. Although the Elgars visited the theatre they would not have seen the actual play, which had previously been performed in 1890 when Thomas Cook made arrangements for 6000 British visitors to see it.

In 1889 the Bavarians had decided that something must be done to improve the dangerous road from Garmisch to Oberammergau. An English lady, Mary Trench, after attending the 1890 play and presumably staying in and travelling from the vicinity of Garmisch, reported that a "magnificent new road, one long zig-zag, had been made in 1889".[7] This road was, in fact, macadamised and eighteen feet wide; no doubt the Elgars and their party used it for their 1893 visit.

To reach Oberammergau by road in 1893, the Elgars would have passed through Ettal. In the Birthplace collection there is a postcard which Alice sent home from Ettal and, although there is no mention of a visit in Alice's diary, in Edward's notebook there is a brief record of a visit to Ettal Kloster in 1893. Robert Anderson writes that "Elgar took the old mule track to the Benedictine Kloster of Ettal."[8] He would have admired the baroque splendour of the interior and he recalls how he heard the Ettal organ being played and remarks on the frescoes in the dome with the 400 figures worshipping the Trinity.[9]

---

[6] Quoted in Moore, Jerrold Northrop: *Edward Elgar - Letters of a Lifetime* (Oxford, Clarendon Press, 1990) p 45

[7] Bentley, James: *Oberammergau and the Passion Play* (Penguin Books, 1984) p 56

[8] Anderson, Robert: *Elgar* (Master Musicians Series, Dent, 1993) p 27

[9] Anderson notes that Elgar wrote that "Count Pappenheim lives in Ettal": this was the name with which he had signed his "Beethoven Credo" of July 1873.

Garmisch

However, a year later, on Saturday 25 August 1894, Edward and Alice paid another visit to Oberammergau. They travelled by the 9.45 am train to Oberau and took a Stellwagen from there. They found Oberammergau all beflagged and decorated. This was the weekend of the consecration of the new Steinmeyer organ that had been built in the parish church of St Peter and St Paul.[10] They lunched at the Wittelsbacher Hof then attended what was presumably the inaugural organ recital. Afterwards they had coffee and Edward was introduced to the organist who took him back into the church. In Alice's words, "Edward played most 'booful' music". Later they walked back down to Oberau in the twilight and travelled back to Garmisch by the 9.50 pm train.

During the 1894 holiday the Elgars broke into their stay in Garmisch to go south. On Wednesday 14 August they walked to the Partnachklamm, though not by the modern tourist path as this was not constructed by the local alpine club until 1912. Eventually, by walking on some eight miles, they reached Mittenwald where that night they slept at The Post. Mittenwald is a pretty town which Goethe described as a "living picture book". It is situated in the green valley of the Isar, immediately below the towering Karwendel chain. Much of the attractiveness of this town is due to its painted houses. Chalets with bright exteriors, low overhanging eaves and wall frescoes or 'Luftmalerei', many with religious themes, snuggle together in the shadow of rugged peaks. If Thursday 15th had not been a holiday - the Feast of the Assumption of the Blessed Virgin (Maria Himmelfahrt) - they would surely have visited the violin school. However they went to church to hear Mass. The tower of this church exhibits excellent examples of vividly painted Luftmalerei. Church was followed by a drive through the Leutasch Tal and so they passed through a most beautiful mountain valley in the Northern Tyrol. They eventually reached Seefeld, an Austrian town lying between Innsbruck and Mittenwald and nowadays a health resort, surrounded by forest-covered hills and high peaks. Elgar called this "a very lovely, and ever to be remembered, little excursion". Near Seefeld, in Elgar's words, they had "walked across pastures to a curious roman looking chapel - Christ over altar with real hair".[11]

---

[10] It had been reported earlier in the Loisach-Bote of 4 November 1890 that Herr Oberst Ward had written to *The Times* requesting contributions for the new Oberammergau Organ.

[11] Anderson, *op cit*, p 29

The Innsbruck visits of Friday 16 and Saturday 17 August 1894 were mentioned earlier. All that needs to be said now is that on this occasion they travelled from Seefeld by rail and stayed at the Hotel d'Europe. Alice's diary shows how impressed Edward was by his surroundings.

> Much new snow on the mountains, Edward wildly rushing after engines. Lovely effect of sun setting. Lights in snow and the distant peaks.

But on the return journey through the Inn valley, on Sunday 18 August, they saw the procession of the Blessed Sacrament from a window above the main street of Nassereit; Elgar made a note of the chiming bells:

> C, D, F-sharp and B-flat.

On Monday 20 August 1894, the Elgars left Nassereit from where they were able to walk through the Fern Pass, a distance of some 10 -11 miles. They eventually arrived at Lermoos, then travelled back to Garmisch by some form of horse and Stellwagen. On the way, they were able to see the Zugspitze from the road approaching Obermoos.

The next year, 1895, on the way from Innsbruck again, the diaries state that they enjoyed a lovely drive to Garmisch by way of Seefeld and Mittenwald, where they had lunch. They arrived in Garmisch about 5.30pm. The Elgars' earlier travels and exploratory journey had left only 2 weeks, 21 August - 4 September, to spend in Garmisch where, at the Villa Bader, the Slingsby-Bethells accepted the dedication of *From the Bavarian Highlands* choral suite.

However on their return in 1897, for what was to be their last stay in Garmisch, they were able to spend Friday 13 August to Wednesday 1 September again at the Villa Bader.

Chapter Six
The Villa Bader, Karl Bader and the Slingsby-Bethells

The Elgars stayed for all of the Bavarian holidays in Garmisch in the 1890s at the Villa Bader, a guest house/pension kept by Mr and Mrs Henry Slingsby-Bethell. They stayed there for two weeks in 1893, nearly six weeks in 1894, two weeks in 1895 and nearly three weeks in 1897.

In his diary/notebook Elgar gives some account of what life was like at the Villa Bader:[1]

> [The Villa Bader] was in the village of G, in the Bavarian Highlands: under the verandah of the Villa B in the evening was to be found our ideal of peace & rest, &, rising a mile away, the mountains of the long Welterstein (*sic*) range;[2] Curling round at the western end of the precipitous Waxenstein holding in its bosom, the mysterious Höllenthal.
>
> Looking from the house straight across, beyond the wooden houses of the village, pine woods & pastures rise high up in the foreground, above them the bare rock & covering the highest points snow. This does not remain in any quantity in the late summer-time, but.........a storm [may] come: great clouds [cover] the naked peaks for an hour & occasionally the edge somewhat lifted showing the fury of it! later the sun [comes] out & the clouds pass away leaving the pinnacles newly white, gleaming with the purity of virgin snow.
>
> This was what we [look] upon as long as we might in the evening, for the next day the sun [will] mar our picture & the snow [will] again, in great measure, depart. Twinkling lights high up in the mountains appear; the fires of the haymakers who remain on the hillsides all night saving the precious hours which would otherwise be wasted in journeying to the village and back each day.

---

[1] Quoted in Moore, Jerrold Northrop (ed): *Edward Elgar - Letters of a Lifetime* (Oxford, Clarendon Press, 1990) p 44

[2] Wetterstein is the correct spelling.

In The Bavarian Highlands

The occasional postcard such as this one was jointly written and sent to Edward's mother in Worcester:

Villa Bader Garmisch Bavaria
Monday August 6th 1894.

A & I are walking today - very hot and we are resting at this house on a balcony drinking Bier, I need not say; no letters from you yet at which we wonder much. Hope all are well - will write soon. Archbp arrived on Saturday just as jolly as ever. I wish you cd be here   Suddenly it is so lovely, a grilling sun but we hope to be under firs soon.[3]

Then Alice adds:

E looks so well, a straw hat & he bought a delightful cloak in Munich in wh he looks like a magician! The Bethells are nicer than ever.

Much love
Yr
C.A.E.[4]

It is not clear from this postcard at which house they were "resting": the Villa Bader, or one on the route of their walk to the Badersee, from where they returned home through Grainau.

---

[3]   Moore, *op cit*, pp 46-47

[4]   *ibid*

Elgar with hat
(see letter above)
[The Elgar Birthplace Museum]

There were a wide variety of activities. Elgar played golf and relaxed completely, thoroughly enjoying himself. On a "rest day", Saturday 1 September 1894, he played football with the Slingsby-Bethell boys, and then early in September when the weather became very wet they played charades and musical chairs. Tea parties were held and Edward was busy with his camera trying to photograph mountain thunderstorms. There were also festivities and fireworks at the Villa Bader on Saturday 31 August 1895. On Tuesday 3 September 1895, the day before they left for Munich, an Elgar 'benefit' cricket match was organised.

But it was not all games and expeditions. Music was never far from Edward's thoughts even on holiday. Whilst at the Villa Bader in 1895 he received Capel-Cure's draft libretto for *Lux Christi* (*The Light of Life*), and Jerrold Northrop Moore tells us that Edward used much of his free time during his holiday here to sketch music for the blind man's story.[5] "High art" he later called it, because it was written 6000 feet above sea level![6]

During the hurriedly arranged holiday in 1897, the Elgars hired costumes from the Mikado company in order to attend a 'Fancy Ball' on the evening of Wednesday 18 August. Alice thought Edward "very nice" as a Japanese maquata, whilst she went in more orthodox fashion in Bavarian costume. The next day, the 19th, all the family, friends and guests at Garmisch were photographed outside the Villa Bader. This holiday, the last to be spent in Garmisch and Bavaria,[7] ended when the Elgars left for Munich on 1 September. Whenever the Elgars left the Slingsby-Bethells to travel from Garmisch back home via Munich there were always emotional farewells, none more so than in 1897.

The only contemporary photograph of the Villa Bader is that from the Elgar Birthplace Museum collection published on page 105 of Pauline Collett's *An Elgar Travelogue*.

Unfortunately, the reproduction does not have the clarity of the original but, when this photograph is examined using a magnifying glass, it is

---

[5] Moore, Jerrold Northrop: *Edward Elgar - A Creative Life* (Oxford University Press, 1984) p 196

[6] Kennedy, Michael: *Elgar Society Journal* (January 1991) p 25

[7] There were brief visits to Bayreuth in 1902 and Garmisch in 1909.

Elgar in fancy dress, taken the morning after a Villa Bader party
[The Elgar Birthplace Museum]

possible to read the smaller lettering. 'VILLA BADER', in large letters, is painted on two boards or banners hung on either side of the two upper windows. It is, however, the lettering above the two upper windows which is important. It reads:

ERBAUT
18   KARL BADER   86

The original photograph suggests that it was taken in winter when snow was on the ground, so it is reasonable to suggest that the photograph was sent to Elgar and not actually taken by him.

These details raise the question as to why a house, apparently built in 1886 by Karl Bader, was being run as a guest house by an English family in 1893, some seven years later. The original possibility was that Karl Bader was simply a builder, speculating on the growth of tourism in Garmisch which accompanied the arrival of the railway, increased interest in mountain climbing and of course the increasing appeal of the Oberammergau passion play.

My wife and I had first tried to locate the Villa Bader in 1984. We had been told that an attempt to find it had been made in 1970 but that it was unsuccessful and it was presumed that the house had been demolished, drastically altered or its name had been changed.[8]

The local tourist office originally told us that the Haus Karl Bader, Marienplatz 7 (no 43),[9] in the centre of the 'village', was the house of the family Bader. This later turned out to be correct, but clearly, unless it had been severely altered, it was not the Villa Bader where Elgar stayed. It now had two shops on the ground floor facing the Marienplatz and HAUS KARL BADER in bold letters just below the two upper windows. The Slingsby-Bethell's Villa Bader appears much wider than the Haus Karl Bader : the former had five first floor windows at the front, whereas this Haus had only three. Four first floor windows were at the side; now there are five. In August 1996, whilst preparing a presentation for the London branch of the Elgar Society, I sent a further enquiry, this time to the Garmisch Partenkirchen Heimat Museum. By an enormous stroke of luck the museum passed my enquiry to Herr Martin Schöll, a local historian. He is a specialist in research into the older houses of Garmisch-Partenkirchen and is the author of the book *Hauser die nicht mehr stehen. Originale die nicht mehr leben* (trans. *Houses which no longer stand. Originals which no longer live*).

Amongst other things in this book there are some lovely photographs of old Garmisch and its houses which convey to the modern reader some idea of the Garmisch the Elgars knew and loved. Martin Schöll explained that it is necessary to know something of the Bader family history and their houses as background to the location of the Villa Bader.

Karl Bader's birthplace was Das Alte Gasthaus zur Traube (House No 95): The Old Guest House of the Grapes. This house was originally built in 1512 as a tavern and mail station. In 1889 the building was renamed Hotel zur Post and in 1891 became Clausings Post Hotel,

---

[8] Personal communication from Pauline Collett.

[9] In Elgar's time there and for some time into the twentieth century, houses in Garmisch were recorded by numbers rather than by street/road names and numbers.

Agnes and Karl Bader [Martin Schöll]

Garmisch, the name by which it is still known and still to be found in the centre of Garmisch at Marienplatz 12.

By 1874, Karl Bader was living in house No 222 (now Fruhlingstrasse 35) with his mother's sister Walburg Resch (née Wurmer). In 1875 Karl Bader's family sold Das Alte Gasthaus zur Traube and moved to Marienplatz 9 (No 44), a semi-detached house adjoining No 43. In 1876, Karl Bader married Agnes Klarwein (1848-1925). At the time of the marriage, she owned and lived in Haus No 152b, then called the Villa Wittelsbach. It was half of a semi-detached house, originally built about 1650. As a result of the union the house came into the joint ownership of Karl and Agnes. A little while later, as Karl's business interests prospered, he acquired (probably in 1886, the date of the death of the last resident) House No 152a.

Karl Bader became something of a business man, one of the first - if not the first - in the village of Garmisch, which was now emerging from its traditional agrarian economy. He certainly had many interests. He was

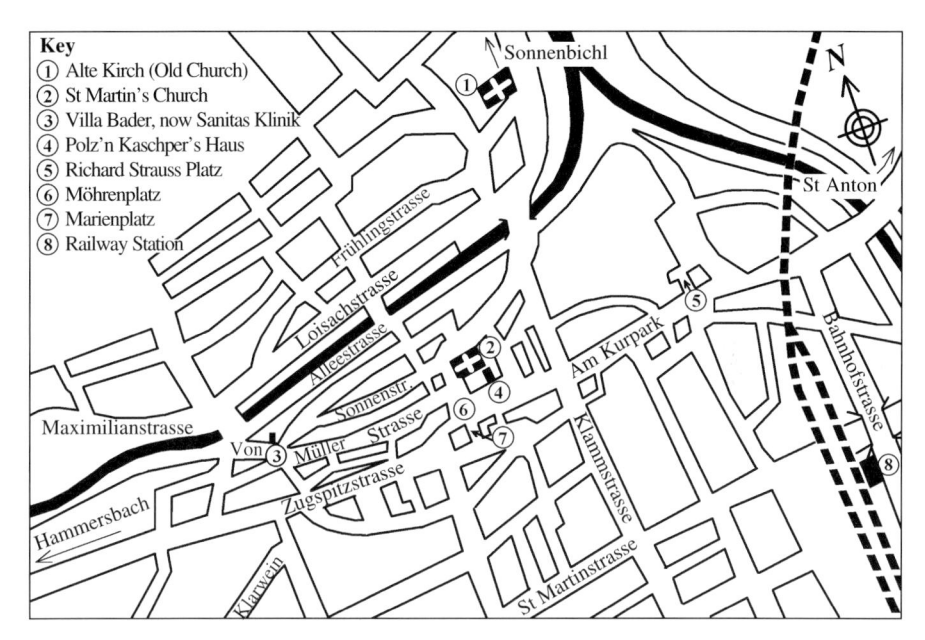

Street map of Garmisch

a bookbinder by trade and training. He also made wallpaper. He sold bread and, in fact, was the 'bread controller' at the brothaus (now the post office next to the Alte Apotheke in Garmisch). He also sold clothes and at that time was one of the few people in Garmisch to have anticipated the possibilities of the growing tourist trade.[10]

The proceeds of his business activities were to be invested in property. He also needed a house in the centre of Garmisch commensurate with his growing status. So in 1883 Karl Bader built himself a fine new house, No 43 (now Marienplatz 7), on land where the former house No 43 had stood before its demolition.[11] Then in 1886 (the date on the front

---

[10] I am indebted to Martin Schöll for this information in several personal communications and interviews. Other information is derived from Garmisch Census Return sheets 461 and 463.

[11] This is the house "Haus Karl Bader" which the tourist office had previously told us was the Villa Bader. It was, of course, the Bader family home but not the Villa Bader where the Elgars' stayed with the Slingsby-Bethells in 1893 and later.

of the Villa Bader photograph) Karl built a new house behind the older former semi-detached houses Nos 152a and 152b. These were then altered and divided into apartments. Now the original house became No 152a and the Villa Karl Bader (later Villa Bader), whilst the new-built house behind became No 152b. 1889 saw the arrival of Henry Slingsby-Bethell in Garmisch to lease the Villa Bader as a pension.[12]

It has been suggested that in the 1890s Karl Bader probably needed to supplement his financial resources in order to engage in more commercial and building operations. So, having inherited house no 222 (Frühlingstrasse 35) on the death of his aunt, Walburga Resch, he sold house no 152 - the Villa Bader (now Von Mullerstrasse 12) to Henry Slingsby-Bethell who then renamed it the Villa Bethell. By 1950 this house had been renamed Bernriederhof and was still in use as a guest house; but, before this time, it is believed that some five or six owners had used its guest-house facilities. Today the Villa Bader is still standing. It is now the Sanitas Klinik at 12 Von Mullerstrasse.

The Villa Bader pension was run by Henry Slingsby-Bethell when the Elgars first stayed with him and his wife in Garmisch in 1893. Henry was 55 years old, having been born in London on 15 November 1838.[13] His wife Sarah (née Sarah Hovenden Macleane) was a year younger, having been born on 7 July 1839, in Tanjore, India.[14] They were married in December 1860 and the marriage was registered in the Cardiff district.[15] There were several children in the family. In March 1876 the birth of Eustace Vincent was registered at Lewisham in south east London.[16] It was Eustace, then 17 years old, who met the Elgars at Garmisch station in 1893. Mary (possibly Margaret Mary Marke née Bethell) met the Elgars on 13 August 1897. Tracing her birthdate and birthplace has presented problems, there being three possibilities:

---

[12] See letter from Henry Slingsby-Bethell dated 10 June 1904 to Garmisch Building Control Office.

[13] Letter to Garmisch Building Control Office dated 10 June 1904.

[14] *ibid*

[15] *Index of National Statistics* 11a 362 and 11a 422

[16] *op cit*, 1d 1031

The Villa Bader, Karl Bader and the Slingsby-Bethells   69

Above :
A contemporary photograph of Garmisch House 152 - The Villa Bader - where the Elgars stayed with the Slingsby-Bethells
[The Elgar Birthplace Museum]

Below :
Bernriederhof Guest House - Garmisch House No 152, as the Villa Bader had become by 1951.
[Martin Schöll]

Above : The Villa Bader today, now the Sanitas Klinik
Below : The view along von Mullerstrasse past the Villa Bader/Sanitas Klinik
[Both photos : J W Greaves]

Margaret Mary Bethell's birth was registered at Bath in September 1864; Mary Slingsby-Bethell's birth was registered at Kensington in March 1867 and a Mary Slingsby at Newport, Monmouth in March 1874.[17] Whichever one was our Margaret Mary Bethell, she married Arthur Edmund Levelis Marke, a retired professor who had previously lived at Ross on Wye, Herefordshire. Henry's grandson Phillip Lancelot (Philipp Lanzalot) was born to this couple on 6 September 1898 and his birth was registered in the Garmisch Roman Catholic records the following day. Their address is given as house 152a, - the Villa Bader - and the child's godfather was John Bethell who, in the company of Kelly Brown, had met the Elgars at Garmisch station in 1894.[18]

In 1902 Slingsby-Bethell submitted the plans he had had drawn up for a new, mainly wooden, house No 151, which stood to the left of the Villa Bader, by then renamed the Villa Bethell. Then, on 10 June 1904, Henry Slingsby-Bethell wrote a letter of enquiry to the Garmisch Building Control Office in order to obtain or renew approval of management for his guest-house at Sonnenstrasse 152. This letter indicates that, in addition to the Villa Bethell in Garmisch (Tel Garmisch 71), the Bethells had an address in Rome, at Plazzo Sterbini, 1 Via Babuino (Rome 2448). The heading of the letter also suggests that Bethell was an agent for tickets for the Munich Wagner Operas and also for Bayreuth Operas and the Oberammergau Passion Play.

In the 1904 letter, Henry states that he had run his guest house with a renowned respectability for 15 years, which marks his arrival in Garmisch at 1889. The letter describes the house and requests consent to serve beer and wine to guests and other visitors. The house had 34 rooms, with 60 beds, accommodating approximately 60 guests, all of whom had full board if desired, breakfast, mid-day dinner, and evening meals in the house. Spirits, alcoholic liquors and schnaps were only supplied as medicines! The house, it was claimed, was very well known to the travelling public. The Villa Bader had been leased from Karl Bader between 1889-1897, but in 1897 house 152 was sold to Henry S Bethell and renamed Villa Bethell. Indeed a Fremden Liste (Visitors List) for 19 to 22 August 1893 for the Bethells records "Herr Edward Elgar and Frau, Malvern".

---

[17]   *op cit*, 5c 709, 1a 115 and 11a 236

[18]   Elgar, Alice: Diary entry for 3 August 1894

> From Mr: & Mrs: Henry Slingsby Bethell. *Betriebszeit 1 Juni – 1 Oktober jeden Jahres.* 4
>
> azzo Sterbini. Telegraphic Addresses. Villa Bethell.
> Via Babuino.   Garmisch.
> ROME.   Bethell. Rome.   Bavaria.
>   Bethell. Garmisch. Bavaria.
>   Telephone Rome 2448.   *Garmisch den ... 1904*
>   Garmisch 71.   *10. Juni 1904*
>   1500
>
> Tickets for the Munich Wagner Operas this year;
> also for Bayreuth Operas, and the Ober Ammergau Passion Play.
>
> Ich der Untergezeichnete Henry Slingsby Bethell aus London, geboren 15ten November 1838 von John aus London und meine Frau Sarah Hovenden Macleane geboren 1839 7ten Juli in Tanjore Indien von Arthur Macleane wohnend in Garmisch Villa Bethell Sonnenstrasse 132, ersuchen um die Genehmigung zur Fortführung unserer Fremdenpension, sowie um die Erlaubniss zur Verabreichung von Bier und Wein an unsere Gäste und deren allenfalsige Besuche. Wir nehmen in 34 Zimmern mit 60 Betten ungefähr 60 Gäste und alle auf volle Kost: Frühstück, Mittag und Abendessen im Haus. Geistige Getränke d. h. Liköre und Schnapse werden nur als Arzneimittel an unsere Gäste geliefert. Unser Haus ist für den letzten 15 Jahren an das reisend Publikum sehr bekannt, und besonders berühmt für seine Achtbarkeit.
>
> Hochachtungsvoll Henry S Bethell

Letter from Henry Slingsby-Bethell to the Garmisch building control office seeking permission to run his guest house as a 'holiday home'

[Martin Schöll]

The Villa Bader, Karl Bader and the Slingsby-Bethells

By the end of 1905, community building reports on house 152 had been filed, but by then Henry Slingsby-Bethell was probably living at his Rome house, because when the Elgars visited Rome on 12 February 1907 they stayed with the Slingsby-Bethells.[19] Yet members of the Bethell family stayed on in Garmisch. The 1912 address book records that Eustace Vincent Bethell, now 36 years old, was a guest house owner/pension house keeper living at Sonnenstrasse 151 (now 16 Von Mullerstrasse - the newbuilt wooden chalet). Incidentally the houses in Garmisch were numbered not in street order but on the basis of the entire village. Sarah Bethell (presumably another daughter) lived next door at 152 Sonnenstrasse (now Von Mullerstrasse).

It is reasonable to assume that when the First World War broke out in 1914, the Slingsby-Bethells were expelled in company with the rest of the English community. However, a postcard of house 151, taken in 1921, records that it was owned by an Irene Bethell and was being run as a pension.

This account leaves many details about the Slingsby-Bethells to be discovered, and several questions to be answered. One can only speculate about why they went to Garmisch in the first place in 1889. Henry is "sometimes credited as Captain and sometimes as Colonel."[20] Perhaps, after an army career, keeping a pension in a beautiful part of Europe with a growing tourist trade and an English colony was an attractive retirement career and investment.

Why did the Elgars choose to stay with the Slingsby-Bethells? Dr Jerrold Northrop Moore suggests that they had met the family during the 1892 holiday.[21] Where did they meet them? Certainly not in Garmisch because Minnie Baker took them from Munich directly to Oberstdorf. It is possible that they met during the short stay in Munich on 4 and 5 August 1892, but there is no record of this in Alice's diaries.

---

[19] Anderson, Robert: *Elgar* (Master Musicians Series, Dent, 1993) p 78

[20] Young, Percy M: *Elgar OM, a study of a musician* (Collins, 1955), p 71

[21] Moore, *op cit*, p 175

To Mr & Mrs Henry Slingsby Bethell,
Garmisch, Bavaria.

From the Bavarian Highlands.

Six Choral Songs (S.A.T.B.)

with accompaniment for

PIANO

(or Orchestra)

The words imitated from Bavarian Volkslieder and Schnadahüpfler,
by C. ALICE ELGAR.
The Music composed by

EDWARD ELGAR.

Op. 27.

	Tonic Sol-fa	Old Notation		Tonic Sol-fa	Old Notation
Nº 1. The Dance.	4ᴅ	9ᴅ	Nº 4. Aspiration.	3ᴅ	6ᴅ
Nº 2. False Love.	3ᴅ	9ᴅ	Nº 5. On the Alm.	3ᴅ	9ᴅ
Nº 3. Lullaby.	3ᴅ	9ᴅ	Nº 6. The Marksmen.	6ᴅ	1/6

Tonic Sol-fa (Complete) 1/6 net.   Vocal Score (Complete) 4/- net.
N.B. An edition of this work is published for Male Voice Choirs, arranged by LESLIE WOODGATE
Prices: Nos. 1, 2, 3, & 5, 6d. net each. No. 4, 4d. net. No. 6, 1/- net.

Orchestral parts may be had on hire.   All rights reserved.

LONDON,
JOSEPH WILLIAMS, Limited.
29, Enford Street, W.1

New York : Edw. Schuberth & Co., 11, East 22nd St.

Made and printed in Great Britain.

The cover of the Williams score of From the Bavarian Highlands
[Stainer & Bell]

Chapter Seven

The Bavarian Highlands Music

The frontispiece of *From the Bavarian Highlands* (Opus 27) shows that it was dedicated to Mr and Mrs Henry Slingsby-Bethell, Garmisch, Bavaria. It was eventually published by Joseph Williams in 1896. In its original form as a choral suite of six songs, composed early in 1895, it was presented with accompaniment for piano (or orchestra). Later, in 1897, Elgar orchestrated three of the dances - 'The Dance ', 'Lullaby' and 'The Marksman' - as a concert suite.

After the completion of *The Black Knight* on 26 January, the remainder of 1893 saw Elgar mainly teaching, golfing, and searching around for inspiration. Then, in January 1894, he worked on three solo songs, composed *Sursum Corda* for its première on 8 April, and arranged the Good Friday music from *Parsifal* for small orchestra[1] to be performed in June.

More songs followed and, towards the end of the year, Elgar began to seek out themes on which to compose a really big work. By January 1895 he had become focused on the *Scenes from the Saga of King Olaf*, yet the expected invitation to write a large scale work for a definite festival performance did not materialise, creating something of a hiatus.[2]

Alice Elgar came to the rescue and bridged the gap. She argued that as Novello had accepted several of Edward's part songs, such as *O Happy Eyes*, and *My Love Dwelt in a Northern Land* and including some set to

---

[1]   Moore, Jerrold Northrop: *Edward Elgar - A Creative Life* (Oxford University Press, 1984) pp 177-179

[2]   *ibid*

her words, such as *Fly Singing Bird* and *The Snow*, further verses inspired by and recalling their shared Bavarian holiday experience might indicate a way forward.[3] The holidays in the Bavarian highlands of 1892, 1893 and 1894 were ideal inspiration, especially as a musical focus emerged from the memories of the Schuhplättler[4] dancing and Volkslieder singing, recalling with great happiness evenings spent at Der Drei Mohren inn in Garmisch.

It is suggested by some that Alice had freely translated the poems from the words of the Bavarian Volkslieder and Schnadahüpfler into English. Yet it is clear that Edward and Alice were responsible for the composition of the poems' words[5] although, as the frontispiece to the score reminds us, they were composed in imitation of the Bavarian songs and dances.

It has been suggested that the Elgars' creativity was stirred by scenes, pictures and books. Undoubtedly this was an important factor but, when one adds the vivid holiday experiences, there was a conjunction of circumstances that acted as a stimulus. So it was in the composition of "The Bavarians", as Alice referred to these holidays and the resultant song cycle. This does not seem to have been affected by some of the real life experiences which caused her some trepidation. For example, she had no head for heights and she was very fearful of having to cross a mountain stream on a wooden foot bridge without a handrail.[6] Alice's diaries, as written during the holidays, suggest that she did not always accompany Edward and friends on the more adventurous walks. Thus, at Einodsbach in 1892, it was Minnie Baker and Edward who walked up to the snowline. The implication is that Alice stayed below.

Nevertheless Alice was most impressed by the beauty of the Bavarian scenery, as was Edward. This and other holiday experiences produced songs which exude a happiness reflecting the carefree atmosphere of

---

[3] Moore, *op cit*, p 185

[4] Usually in the Elgarian literature spelt "Schuhplatt'l". The correct term is, however, Schuhplättler.

[5] Young, Percy M: *Alice Elgar: Enigma of a Victorian Lady* (Dennis Dobson, 1978) p 118

[6] Young, *op cit*, p 118

the holidays, and their affinity with Bavarian life. Indeed, apart from the occasional indiscretions and rebukes mentioned by Rosa Burley, together with observation of the appropriate Victorian formalities, it was a blissfully happy time for the Elgars' marriage after the relative discomfort of the early years in London. The songs and the co-operation involved in their composition suggest a compatibility and spirituality in the Elgars' relationship which is much more than mere expression of delight in holiday experiences.[7]

So it is in the spirit of the songs that they are more than just imitation of the Bavarian models. They are clearly not in the vogue of the Elgarian noble melancholy but the product of one of the happiest periods of the Elgars' lives.

Although Alice is often given credit for the text of the songs, Dr Percy Young gives convincing evidence that Alice and Edward worked together on these pieces, a long process of "verbal sublimation". He traces the development of the text of the songs through various extant drafts that bear marks of frequent revision and annotation by each partner.

The account of how the texts of the songs were developed[8] is an enlightening experience to read and one which shows how the Elgars co-operated to achieve the aim of providing a "vehicle for music", with "its several attempts at shaping and re-shaping" which "show clearly how the search for workable rhythmic patterns and for phrase continuity proceeded". Whilst "it is not possible to place all the drafts of pieces in chronological order with absolute certainty........... the manner in which words move towards finality may be inferred from the alterations and modifications".[9]

At the conclusion of the joint enterprise of composing the texts, the words of the songs were copied by Alice on to the backs of sheets of music manuscript paper headed:

---

[7] *ibid*

[8] Young, *op cit*, pp 118-138

[9] The origins of the primary sources of these drafts is not always clear in Dr Young's book but one must assume from the introduction that they are taken from papers given to him by Elgar's daughter Carice, later Mrs Elgar-Blake.

Words for six Bavarian Partsongs
for Chorus and Orchestra
Music by Edward Elgar

and the title page bore an inscription to E E with a dedication from C A E dated 5 March 1895.[10]

As far as the composition of the *Bavarian Highlands* music is concerned, Dr Jerrold Northrop Moore has shown that although "Alice's poems might be separable", overall the songs had a unity; Elgar's "keenness for larger expression led him to interrelate and develop themes from one song to the next". After giving clear examples of this process, Dr Moore comments that "the vocal figures betrayed their instrumental origins". So many spirited variations and developments were indications of "Edward's power to expand his music from the simplest beginnings. Vocal counter point and orchestral polyphonies engaged one another without overreaching the innocent happiness that had brought them together".[11]

Elgar completed the songs in March and early April 1895. From the first mention of the project in the diary, the composition was nearing completion in under six weeks.[12] On 25 March, Edward played the songs, as they had by then been composed, to Isobel Fitton and her sister Hilda, who had holidayed briefly with the Elgars at Garmisch in 1894. The first five Bavarian Highlands songs in vocal score had been taken to London on 28 March and deposited with Berthold Tours, Novello's music editor. The final song needed more work on account of its complex structure, but this too was despatched, with the following letter, on 10 April:

> Dear Sirs,
>
> By this post (registered) I send you No 6 of the set of six part songs for the chorus & orchestra completing the set. Mr Tours kindly took charge of Nos 1-5 which I left with him when I called at your establishment ten days ago.

---

[10] *ibid*

[11] Moore, *op cit*, p 185

[12] *ibid*

The Bavarian Highlands Music

> The collective title From the Bavarian Highlands is intended to go on each number - there are subsidiary titles also. My idea was that the set should be published together in book form & that they should be also procurable separately.
>
> Nos 1,3 & 6 wd make a very useful Suite for orchestra alone, or for piano - duet or solo.
>
> I submit the work to you with confidence as I believe from the character of the music it will find easy acceptance in many quarters.
>
> I shall be much obliged by an early reply,
>
> Believe me
Faithfully yours
Edward Elgar
>
> P.S. The words only are partially arranged (imitated) from Volkslieder - the music is my own.[13]

But the songs were not accepted by Novello. The letter reproduced above was annotated "? Saleable. No 6 is the best. Nos 1 & 3 next NO." The rejection letter, though polite, cast doubt on their saleability in any form.

So after the 1895 Bavarian holiday, Elgar sought publishers until, on 11 December 1895, the songs were accepted, after some hesitation, by the firm of Joseph Williams, a near neighbour of Novello.[14]

> 24 Berners St, London W.
> December 11 1895
>
> Dear Sir,
> In regard to your Bavarian music I shall be pleased to accept it on the following terms.
>   2½d royalty on all pianoforte arrangements
>   no royalty on the orchestral arrangements
>   & 3/- per 100 on the part songs, separately.
>   The usual number of free copies for professional use, review etc.
>
> Faithfully yours

Joseph Williams F.W. [15]

---

[13] Moore, Jerrold Northrop: *Elgar and his publishers* (Clarendon Press. Oxford, 1987) p 27

[14] Moore, *op cit*, p 30

[15] *ibid*

It is not quite clear to which "orchestral arrangements" this letter refers. Thus Nos 1, 3, and 6 for orchestra alone were not set until Autumn 1897. According to Pauline Collett, the first performance of *From the Bavarian Highlands* "took place at Worcester on 21 April 1896 in its original version for four part chorus and piano accompaniment."[16]

The alternative orchestral accompaniment was not written until "later that year". However, Dr Moore states "During a few days in late February and early March [1896], he turned aside to correct the Joseph Williams vocal score proofs of *From the Bavarian Highlands* and to orchestrate them for the first performance on 21 April in Worcester".[17] An interesting problem to be explained by those who believe that the composition of the piano and the orchestral versions proceeded side by side!

Indeed, some interest has, at times, emerged over this alternative view. Undoubtedly Elgar's intention always was to produce an orchestral accompaniment for the songs, a view that John Knowles forcibly argues in his review of a recording[18] of *From the Bavarian Highlands* on page 20 of the January 1982 edition of the Elgar Society Journal.

> I have never been able to accept the oft-quoted assertion that the version of the Bavarian Highlands songs with piano accompaniment is the original, and I hope the appearance of this première recording of the orchestral version will lay that ghost for ever. There is ample documentary evidence that it was Elgar's practice to conceive his music orchestrally from the outset, rather than begin at the keyboard and only later orchestrate it. Why should this work be any different? Indeed, clear corroborative evidence in this case comes in a letter Elgar wrote to Novello on 10 April 1895.
>
> At this stage he had just finished the piano score but had not yet started on the orchestral parts, and yet he refers to the set as "six part songs for chorus and orchestra". It is true that they were first performed with piano, and first appeared in print with the piano part, but surely this was a case of expediency rather than design.

It must, of course, be accepted that Elgar always intended to orchestrate the songs but the "simultaneous" argument does need to be balanced against at least one chronological caveat. The statement in the letter of 10 April 1895 to Novello need be no more than a statement of

---

[16] Collett, Pauline: *An Elgar Travelogue* (Thames Publishing, 1983) p 110

[17] Moore, *op cit*, p 31

[18] Bournemouth Symphony Chorus and Sinfonietta.

intent. Dr Moore suggests that orchestration took place in late February - early March 1896[19] so there was at least an interval of 10-11 months between completing the vocal score and its orchestration.

Fortunately this argument is not essential to John Knowles' contention that "certainly the work seems bigger and more important in its orchestral dress", for many of those features of Elgar's orchestral style, which he was to develop to such heights later on, are there if only, at this stage, comparatively immature. For example, one has only to listen to the orchestral version to appreciate the clarity of the scoring. Perhaps the Wagnerian experiences were as yet too recent to have had an influence; they were still in the process of being absorbed.

Certainly there is little if any of the nobilmente or melancholy we associate with the later, perhaps greater, works. *From the Bavarian Highlands* may not be typical Elgar, but they were composed by a man Rosa Burley describes as being very happy and contented on his holiday in Garmisch and Munich. The "Bavarians" reflect this side of an Elgar who is relaxed and entering into the joyous spirit of the people amongst whom he felt "at home".

Most authors nowadays refer to the suite of songs as *Scenes from the Bavarian Highlands*. The frontispiece of Opus 27 refers to the title of the songs only as *From the Bavarian Highlands* but there have been several variations used in the literature.

In 1933 Basil Maine, on page 72 of his *Life of Elgar*, refers to the work as a choral suite *From the Bavarian Highlands* whilst in 1937 Mrs Richard Powell (Dorabella), on page 8 of *Memories of a Variation*, refers to the work as *Scenes from the Bavarian Highlands*. This seems to be the first time that *Scenes from the Bavarian Highlands* had been used. In 1955 Diana McVeagh, on page 138 of *Edward Elgar - his Life and Music*, refers to the work as *From the Bavarian Highlands* - six choral songs with orchestra. In 1973 Percy Young, on page 77 of *Elgar O.M.*, uses the title *Songs from the Bavarian Highlands*, and repeats the use of this title in *Alice Elgar, Enigma of a Victorian Lady* (page 134). However, in the index to this book, Percy Young shortens this to *From the Bavarian Highlands*.

---

[19] Moore, *op cit*, p 212

In 1968 Michael Kennedy, on page 58 of *Portrait of Elgar*, uses *Scenes from the Bavarian Highlands*, as does Jerrold Northrop Moore in 1984 on page 187 of *Edward Elgar - a Creative Life*. However, in his letter to the publishers on page 27 of *Elgar and his Publishers*, Elgar clearly refers to the work as *From the Bavarian Highlands* - the title which Dr Moore uses in his commentary on the letter in that book.

There does seem to be some confusion over the title of the work and this confusion raises several questions. Why is Elgar's title not now in general use, when referring to this work? How did the word *Scenes* creep in to the title? As far as one can see Dorabella was the first author to introduce the word. In doing so, was she confusing *From the Bavarian Highlands* with one of the next major works that Elgar wrote - *Scenes from the Saga of King Olaf*?

It may be that authors following Dorabella have considered adding *Scenes* because each of the six songs is given a subtitle, commemorating some particular place or "scene" in the vicinity of Garmisch. However in Dr Percy Young's description of Alice's manuscripts, No 1, 'The Dance (Sonnenbichl)' began life with the subtitle 'Zugspitze - Garmisch'; then comes 'Zugspitze, Zum Husaren, (Graseck)'; then 'Im Leutasch Thal' before Elgar finally decided upon 'Sonnenbichl'.[20]

Indeed, a textual examination of some of Alice's poems shows that their words and content have little to do with the places named in the subtitles. Furthermore, the belief that the places named in the subtitles were favoured haunts of the Elgars must be subject to some doubt. Thus song No 1, 'The Dance', really had nothing to do with Sonnenbichl. Elgar wrote that Sonnenbichl was a wooden gasthaus in the mountains and a favourite beer resort of his. But Elgar saw the dancing - the Bavarian Schuhplättler dances - in the local inn, Der Drei Mohren, and it is not clear when Elgar actually went to Sonnenbichl, as Alice's diaries do not mention it as such.

The evidence in Alice's diaries would seem to suggest that the places indicated in the sub-titles were not all among the "scenes" most visited. Some of the more frequent excursions - for example, to the Riessersee (six times) and the Badersee (five times) - are not used as sub-titles. On the other hand, St Anton, which is used, was visited three or four times

---

[20] Young, *op cit*, p 124

The wooden guesthouse at Sonnenbichl, a place at which Elgar liked to drink [Martin Schöll]

and so fully justifies its inclusion. The other sub-titles - for example, Hammersbach - is recorded as having been visited only twice whilst Wamberg and Murnau appear to have been visited only once.

'The Dance' undoubtedly echoes Bavarian folk music with a simple tune in a rather jolly allegretto. Basil Maine writes[21] that 'The Dance' is the most striking music and is a study in those hearty, muscular rhythms which are characteristic of the dances of mountain folk, an expression of the irrepressible high spirits as the rustic couples hasten to the dance, for which only mountain air could be an excuse. Elgar, according to Basil Maine, tries to bring his vocal into line with his instrumental style.

Song No 2, 'False Love ', is sub-titled 'Wamberg. ' Wamberg is still a small, rather isolated village up in the hills on the western side of Garmisch. According to Alice's diary, the Elgars visited Wamberg just once, on 30 August 1894. The song tells a story of frustrated love, which grew up in the Spring, but is rejected for the sake of another.

---

[21] Maine, Basil: *Elgar; his life and music* (G Bell and Sons, 1933) p 223

Above : Wamberg, photographed here in 1890, the village in the hills near Garmisch which gave its name to the subtitle of song no 2; Below : Hammersbach in 1910 [Both photos : Martin Schöll]

Soon "my maiden true" has another lover at the door and sadly the girl is unfaithful. "It is a simple story of a maiden, lover and rival without which many nineteenth century lieder could never have been written."[22] It is a story not peculiar to Wamberg.

Song No 3, 'Lullaby', has as its subtitle 'In Hammersbach'. Hammersbach and Grainau villages, to the south-east of Garmisch, were visited on two, possibly three, occasions. It is a slumber song of touching simplicity as the devoted mother resists the lure of the faraway zither in order to protect and care for her beloved son. "It is a graceful wistful invention in which the blend of vocal and orchestral writing produces a delightful effect."[23]

The idea for Song No 4 does seem to have originated from three or four visits to the pilgrimage chapel of St Anton on the lower slopes of the Wank mountain near Partenkirchen. Visits are recorded in Alice's diary as having been made on 8 and 9 August 1893 and 11 August 1894, and perhaps later, in 1897. In a way, the idea for Song No 4 and its subtitling is quite appropriate to the mood of the music. 'Aspiration bei Sankt Anton' is an almost hymn-like expression of God's protecting hand, incorporating a prayer that our souls may be properly guided. Its solemnity in quadruple time does seem to create a quasi-religious atmosphere.

Hoch Alp, the place named in the subtitling for Song No 5, 'On the Alm', was a mountain pasture to the south of Hammersbach where, in summer, a peasant girl would live in a hut to tend the grazing cattle. Unfortunately, there is no mention in the diaries of a visit to Hoch Alp, which is some 1705m above sea level and nowadays is reached by cable car. The song gives an idyllic picture of life in the mountain meadows, a mellow bell rings across clover-blossomed fields, the sun shines, swallows and chamois abound and the young man knows that the love of a flaxen-haired sweetheart awaits him on the Hoch Alp. There is a particularly happy contrast between the quasi-religious atmosphere of the fourth and the lyrical writing of the fifth song. In the latter, voices and instruments are again harmoniously related and the opening orchestral melody appears later in the higher voice parts as the burden of the song.

---

[22] *op cit*, pp 223-224

[23] *ibid*

The Hoch Alm, 1700 metres above sea level [Martin Schöll]

The sixth song, 'The Marksman (Bei Murnau)', is believed to refer to a shooting club's activities on the Staffelsee, a large lake near Murnau, a town to the north of Garmisch which the Elgars visited on 11 and 12 September 1894. The song is a vigorous portrayal of a shooting party, hunting out in the hills, with the sound of the crack of rifle shot and cheers after a hit clearly heard. At the close of the day the sun sets in the west and the triumphant hunters return homeward with their prizes through meadows sweet with new-mown hay. It is a spirited song which brings the songs to a rousing finale.

The first performance of *From the Bavarian Highlands* was given in Worcester by the Worcester Festival Choral Society on 21 April 1896 at the Public Hall. Pauline Collett writes that it was "in its original version for four-part chorus and piano accompaniment".[24] However, Dr Moore states that "During a few days in late February and early March he turned aside to correct the Joseph Williams vocal score proofs of *From the Bavarian Highlands* and to orchestrate them for their first performance on 21 April in Worcester".[25]

---

[24] Collett, *op cit*, p 110

[25] Moore, *op cit*, p 31

The Bavarian Highlands Music

There were also informal performances. On 9 July 1897, Dorabella, in remembering the Elgars' visit to her family, recalls that they had music, including *From the Bavarian Highlands*. She remembered how much she liked the Bavarians and after Elgar had played the 'Lullaby' (In Hammersbach), she could not help interrupting and expressing a wish that she would like to convey her love for the music in dance. Elgar, apparently, was very much in agreement with the suggestion and the idea was tried out. This pleased Elgar greatly and the parts of the dance were rehearsed again to fit in some steps more suitably. Later on Dorabella was requested to dance the first section of the Bavarian music on several occasions at Malvern.[26]

Following Elgar's setting of Nos 1, 3 and 6 for orchestra, entitled *Three Bavarian Dances*, attempts to interest August Manns in performing the *Bavarian Highlands* songs at the Crystal Palace resulted in an offer to play three of them. Seventy-seven-years-old Sir George Grove was in attendance at both the Friday and Saturday concerts, 22 and 23 October 1897, and after hearing the *Three Bavarian Dances* he wrote to Elgar expressing the hope that he would compose some more dances immediately because they were so fresh and tuneful. Sir George liked them better than *King Olaf*.

It seems that Sir George had been loaned Alice's copy of *From the Bavarian Highlands* as in the same letter he advised that he would be returning it by post the next day. Sir George also wrote to Alice expressing his appreciation of "that lively heartfelt music".[27] Incidentally this copy of Alice's may well be the one in the Birthplace Museum. To her copy of *From the Bavarian Highlands* vocal score, Alice added photographs, for example the St Anton pilgrimage chapel and a view of Partenkirchen from St Anton fixed opposite the song 'Aspiration.' Later this score came into the possession of Lady Boult who donated it to the Museum in 1983.

The next performance of the *Bavarian Highlands* music took place on 11 November 1897 with the Leeds Choral Union, one of the best choirs in the country. This was Elgar's first public performance in Leeds and

---

[26] Powell, Mrs Richard: *Edward Elgar - Memories of a Variation* (Methuen & Co, 3rd ed, 1949) p 8

[27] Young, Percy M: *Elgar OM, a study of a musician* (Collins, 1955)

the concert included four songs *From the Bavarian Highlands*. The local newspaper, the Mercury, reported that "Mr Elgar is quite the most promising native musician of the day and now that an introduction has been effected, we trust to be able to record many similar visits to the city in future".

Indeed another visit was paid to Leeds on 15-17 February 1898 for a performance of four of the songs. On 19 April there was a performance of *From the Bavarian Highlands* at Hereford, while the three orchestral dances were played at the Queen's Hall on 11 October and the concert of the Worcestershire Philharmonic included the songs on 1 November. They were given again at Worcester in 1903 on 28 April.

If reaction to *From the Bavarian Highlands* from Sir George Grove and the Leeds Mercury had been quite favourable, by the time Basil Maine came to comment on the work, in 1933, the reaction was more guarded:

> The Choral Suite From the Bavarian Highlands (Opus 27) was not likely at its first appearance to add greatly to Elgar's reputation. Pleasing as its holiday mood and facile invention were, it gave no certain sign of genius's touch.[28]

He thought that the second and sixth songs lacked the inherent merit of the others, although the latter can be said to carry out the function of a spirited finale and to provide a satisfactory counterpart to the vivacious dance at the beginning.

One of the first post-1939-45 war biographers of Elgar was rather critical and dismissive in her assessment of *From the Bavarian Highlands*.[29] But then at that time she obviously had not had the opportunity of hearing the two recent recordings which undoubtedly bring out the orchestral brilliance of the work. In this early review the songs were described as companionable - whatever that means - fresh, lively, tuneful - which they certainly are - and devoid of Elgar's personality. If one means by this his noble melancholy, it is agreed; but if, as has been suggested earlier, the way his personality reacted to the enjoyment of his Bavarian holidays, hardly so. 'On the Alm' and 'Aspiration' were described as "moods" which usually demand a personal response but

---

[28] Maine, *op cit*, p 72

[29] McVeagh, Diana M: *Edward Elgar; his life and music* (J M Dent, 1955) p 139

which here are characterless. 'On the Alm' for this writer conveys an idyllic mood in which the young man's love for his recent sweetheart is happily placed in a picturesque and romantic setting. 'Aspiration' is suitably in hymn-like harmony with the quasi-religious mood it seeks to convey and is appropriate to the venue that inspired it.

By 1982 we have Hans Keller writing in the *Musical Times*[30] more favourably:

> How many professional readers, how many amateurs are familiar with *From the Bavarian Highlands*? Not even the Elgar literature (so far as I know it and including the new Grove article on the composer) contains any reference to the work's outstanding characteristics. For one thing, that is to say, there is its emphatically central European idiom untouched by Elgar's later (rather than congenital) modalism whose intricate subtlety was to include a civilized internationalization of nationalism. For another thing, show me one other work, sets of waltzes apart, whose four or more movements confine themselves to triple time. The only departure, if departure you can call it, is the compound triple time of the sixth and last choral song: three beats rule or rather are ruled right to the end which, nevertheless, shocks by its all too early arrival, so rich is the rhythmic variety within triplicity. Yet offhandedness is all I can find about the piece in the Elgar literature, if anything. Granted the style is light, the substance slight; perhaps you have to be not an Elgar specialist in order to perceive, none the less, a perdurable touch of elemental genius. Not all is forgiven.

It is to be hoped that we have moved on since 1982 and have benefited from the newer biographies and Elgarian literature. For example, Robert Anderson[31] suggests that the songs *From the Bavarian Highlands* hint at the melodic freshness and rhythmic piquancy of Dvořák. He believes that much of the music has "carefree spontaneity" but it is "subtly wrought". By 1895 Elgar was already master of the thematic processes that would produce the *Enigma Variations* four years later. Thus in 'The Dance' the strong rhythms and brisk music suggest the enthusiasm with which the peasants hurry to the dancing, whilst in 'False Love' the cross rhythms of the introduction give way to a serene melody praising the coming of Spring and hints of late melancholy are expressed in the sadness with the girl's infidelity. In 'Lullaby' the contralto line expresses a slumber song with appropriate simplicity. 'Aspiration', in quadruple time, is the most solemn yet. In 'On the Alm' the device of unaccompanied men's voices is used to

---

[30] *Musical Times* Vol 123, February 1982, p 119

[31] Anderson, *op cit*, p 180

describe the girl tending the cattle on the hill pasture, while the Murnau huntsmen have suitably robust music in the ebullient finale. So a variety of six themes, highly individualised, is thus conveyed skilfully with the Bavarian music supporting so convincingly Robert Anderson's assertion of Elgar's competence in thematic composition.[32]

In a book principally concerned with Alice Elgar, Dr Percy Young[33] sums up the position the Elgars had reached in 1896 just after the first performance of *From the Bavarian Highlands* as ending a chapter in their lives. One cannot accept that the composition of the Bavarian music and songs represented the summit of personal fulfilment because that surely came later with the success of the *Enigma*, yet it is true that this was a period of great and mutual happiness. Certainly Alice must have found the recognition of her contribution to the poetic verses of this work very satisfying as she had had literary aspirations since childhood and was convinced of the value of poetry to human emotion and expression. What is certain, and what has emerged from this study, is the pleasure and happiness the Elgars found in working together to produce their musico-poetic impressions of Bavarian life - their "tribute of esteem and affection to my many friends among a noble and simple people".[34]

Furthermore Elgar had arrived at this watershed with only relatively small achievements to show in the pursuit of a career as an established composer: *Froissart*, Serenade for Strings, *The Black Knight*, various songs, *Sursum Corda* and a Sonata for Organ. He was, after all, in the fourth decade of his life with his fortieth birthday approaching. Yet, with the first performance of *From the Bavarian Highlands*, his name was becoming more widely known.

Elgar could now go on with increasing confidence to more success with *The Light of Life* and *Scenes from the Saga of King Olaf*. If he had not exactly arrived, he was well on the way, happily and eagerly supported by Alice on this occasion as he would be throughout the rest of her life.

---

[32]   *ibid*

[33]   Young, *op cit*, p 135

[34]   Elgar's programme note for the première of the work quoted in Anderson, *op cit*, p 180

Appendix A
Bibliography

'Adam' Colour Guide : *Garmisch - Partenkirchen*
Anderson R : *Elgar* (Master Musicians' Series) (London : J M Dent, 1993)
Bentley J : *Oberammergau and the Passion Play* (Penguin, 1984)
Burley R and Carruthers F C : *Edward Elgar - The Record of a Friendship*
  (London: Barrie and Jenkins, 1972)
Collett P : *An Elgar Travelogue* (London: Thames Publishing 1983)
Edwards Lee M : *Sir Hubert von Herkomer: English or German painter*
  (Newes Stadtmuseum, Landsberg am Lech)
Elgar A : Diaries 1892-7 (Barber Institute, University of Birmingham)
Elgar E : Diaries and holiday notes (Elgar Birthplace Museum, Broadheath)
Hodgkins (ed) : *The Elgar Society Journal*
Kennedy M : *Portrait of Elgar* (3rd Edition) (Oxford University Press, 1987)
McVeagh D M : *Edward Elgar: His Life and Music* (London: J M Dent, 1955)
Maine B : *Elgar: His Life and Works* (London: G Bell and Sons, 1933)
Moore J N : *Edward Elgar, A Creative Life* Oxford
  (Oxford University Press, 1984)
Moore J N : *Elgar and His Publishers - letters of a creative life* (Vol 1)
  Oxford (Clarendon Press, 1987)
Moore J N : *Edward Elgar - Letters of a Lifetime*
  (Oxford University Press, 1990)
Monk R (Ed) : *Elgar Studies* (Aldershot: Scolar Press, 1990)
Powell Mrs Richard : *Edward Elgar - Memories of a Variation*
  (Oxford University Press, 1949)
Thoma Eugen and Schlegel Paul : *Oberstdorf* (Fussen: Franz Milz)
Young P M (Ed) : *Letters of Edward Elgar and other Writings*
  (London: Bles, 1956)
Young P M : *Elgar O.M. A Study of a Musician* (London: Collins, 1955)
Young P M : *Alice Elgar - Enigma of a Victorian Lady*
  (London: Dennis Dobson, 1978)
- : *Sir Hubert von Herkomer, a Catalogue of the Centenary exhibition
  celebrating his Mutterturm in Landsberg* (Landsberg am Lech, 1988)

Appendix B

Recordings

The following listing includes all releases from complete recordings of the choral songs, with orchestral or piano accompaniment, and of the dances, together with a few historic partial recordings. A number of other recordings, not listed here, have been made of individual pieces, particularly from the dances. Dates shown in square brackets following some releases (eg [2/75]) give the issue of *The Gramophone* magazine in which reviews of the associated release appeared.

From the Bavarian Highlands - Choral Songs (1895)

Sheffield Choir, conductor Henry Coward (recorded 1907)[1]
    Odeon - 44947 (78rpm); 742 (10¾" 78rpm)

Sheffield & Leeds Choirs, conductor Henry Coward[1,2]
    Columbia - 328 (78rpm, released December 1912)

Worcester Cathedral Choir, Frank Wibaut (piano), conductor Christopher Robinson
    Polydor - 2460 239 (LP) [2/75]   Chandos - CHAN 6601 (CD) [9/94]

Scottish Philharmonic Singers, BBC Scottish Symphony Orch, conductor Charles Groves
    BBC - 15656.91802 (CD, recorded Feb 1981, released 1996)

Donald Hunt Singers, Keith Swallow (piano), conductor Donald Hunt
    Abbey - ABY 821 (LP) [6/81]

Bournemouth Sinfonietta Choir & Orchestra, conductor Norman Del Mar
    HMV - ASD 4061 (LP)/TC-ASD 4061 (Cassette) [9/81]
    EMI - CDC 749738-2 (CD) [6/88]; CDM 565129-2 (CD) [7/95]

Exon Singers, Robert Bottone (piano), conductor Christopher Tolley
    Alpha - ACA 515 (LP) [10/83]

CBSO Chorus, Richard Markham (piano), conductor Simon Halsey
    Conifer - CFC 142 (LP) [3/87]/MCFC 142 (Cassette) [11/87]/CDFC 142 (CD) [8/87];
    7560 5517522 (CD, released September 1995)

Tudor Choir of Leicester, Barry Collett (piano)
    Whitetower - ENS 157 (Cassette)

London Symphony Chorus & Orchestra, conductor Richard Hickox
    Chandos - CHAN 9436 (CD) [5/96]

---

[1] - *The Dance*   [2] - *Lullaby*   [3] - *The Marksmen*

Index to Recordings

Bavarian Dances (1896)

Symphony Orchestra, conductor Edward Elgar (recorded HMV Studios, 1914[2,3]/1917[1])
    HMV - 2-0824[1]/2-0519[2]/2-0530[3] (78rpm); D 175[1,2]/D 176[3] (78rpm);
    Pearl - GEM 113 (LP) ; EWE 1 (LP boxed set); GEMM CDS 9951/5 (CD) [9/92]
London Symphony Orchestra, conductor Edward Elgar (recorded 1927[1,2]/1932[3])
    HMV - D 1367 (78rpm)[1,2] [2/28]; DB 1667 (78rpm)[3]; DB 7151 (78rpm)[3];
        HLM 7005 (LP) [3/72]; RLS 713 (LP) [2/75];   EMI - CDS 754564-2 (CD) [2/93]
Royal Symphony Orchestra, conductor Joseph Batten (recorded September 1925)
    Edison Bell - VF 1139/40 (10" 78rpm)
National Symphony Orchestra, conductor Boyd Neel
    Decca - AK 1295/6 (78rpm) [10/49]
London Symphony Orchestra, conductor Lawrance Collingwood
    Columbia - 33SX 1030 (LP) [9/54]; SCD 2036 (7" 45rpm)[1,2] [9/54];
        DX 1914 (78rpm)[1,2] [1/55]; SED 5523 (7" 45rpm)[1,2] [9/55]
Music for Pleasure - MFP 2046 (LP) [8/66]
London Philharmonic Orchestra, conductor Adrian Boult
    Decca - LW 5174 (10" LP) [7/55]; ACL 113 (LP); ECS 646 (LP) [9/72];
        7-1067 (7" 45rpm)[1,2] [7/55]   Belart - 461 359-2 (CD) [9/97]
London Philharmonic Orchestra, conductor Adrian Boult
    HMV - ASD 2356 (LP)/TC-ASD 2356 (Cassette) [3/68]; HQS 1283 (LP) [11/72][3];
        TCC2-POR 54291 (Cassette) [10/85];   ED 291129-1 (LP)/ED 291129-4 (Cassette)
    EMI - CDM 769207-2 (CD) [4/88]
Bournemouth Sinfonietta, conductor Norman Del Mar
    RCA - LRL 1 5133 (LP) [11/76]; RK 11746 (Cassette)
    Chandos - CBR 1016 (LP)/CBT 1016 (Cassette) [6/84]; CHAN 8371 (CD) [8/85];
        CHAN 6544 (CD)/MBTD 6544 (Cassette) [2/92];   CHAN 241/4 (CD) [*2/99]
English String Orchestra, conductor William Boughton (recorded 1988)
    Nimbus - NI 5136 (CD); NI 1769 (CD boxed set) Woolworths - CLASS 7055 (CD)

- **Arrangements for Brass Band**

HM Scots Guards Band, conductor Wood (recorded July 1923)
    Edison Bell - VF 1073/4 (10" 78rpm)
Black Dykes Mills Band, conductor Peter Parkes
    Chandos - BBRD 1031 (LP)/ BBTD 1031 (Cassette) [9/86]; CHAN 8551 (CD) [10/89];
        CHAN 4507 (CD) /BBTD 4507 (Cassette) [9/93]
Grenadier Guards Band, conductor Stuart Watts
    Bandleader - BNC 63006 (Cassette) [3/90]

Index

Allgäuer mountains 13, 33
Audran, Edmond 8
Augsberg 36, 39
Bader, Karl & Agnes 64-68, *66*, 71
Badersee 48, 54, 62, 82
Baker, Mary Frances ('Minnie') 7-10, 15-16, 23, 33-36, 39-42, 73, 76,
Baker, William Meath 7, 35
Bayreuth 8, 11-13, 71
Beethoven, Ludwig van *10*, 11
Berchtesgaden 20
Bingen 17
Birgsau 39, 42
Boult, Lady 87
Brahms, Johannes 7, 16, 30
Breitach river and gorge 41
Bruges 18-19
Brussels 11
Burley, Rosa 8-9, 23, 25-30, 47, 77, 81

Capel-Cure, Rev Edward 63
Cleveland, Ohio 5
Cologne 11, 17-18, 22, 31-32
Constance, Lake 15
Covent Garden 4

Davey, Alice 26-28, 30
Dieppe 11
Dorabella - see Powell, Mrs Richard
Dover 10
Dürer, Albrecht 13-14
Düsseldorf 48
Dvořák, Antonin 89

Eibsee 54
Einodsbach *38*, 39, 42, 76
Elgar Birthplace Museum 40, 53, 58, 63, 87
Elgar, Carice 9, 52-53
Elgar, Edward :
    Black Knight, The 15-16, 75, 90
    Dream of Gerontius, The 1, 48
    Enigma Variations 1, 15, 35, 89-90
    Fly, Singing Bird 76
    Froissart Overture 90
    From the Bavarian Highlands 1, 43, 47, 49-50, 52-54, 60, *74*, 75-90
    King Olaf 75, 82, 87, 90
    Light of Life, The (Lux Christi) 63, 90
    My Love Dwelt in a Northern Land 75
    O Happy Eyes 75
    Organ Sonata 90
    Serenade for Strings 90
    Snow, The 76

Starlight Express, The 54
Sursum Corda 90
Symphony No2 26
Three Bavarian Dances 43, 75, 79, 87
Ettal 58

Fitton, Isobel 51, 78
Flushing 10, 22
Foster-Ward family 49
Frankfurt 18
Freibergsee 40

Garmisch 1, 5, 8, 17-19, 21-22, 31-32, *43*, 43-76, 78, 81-82, 85
Drei Mohren Inn, Die *46*, 47, 76, 82
Marienplatz 44, *45*, 48, 65, 67
Möhrenplatz 45
Polz'n Kashper's Haus 45, *55*
St Martin's church 44-45, 47, *55*
Sanitas Klinik - see Villa Bader
Sonnenstrasse 47, *56*
Villa Bader 1, 54, 60-73, *69-70*
Villa Bethell - see Villa Bader
Goethe, J W von 18, 59
Grafton family 13, 34, 39-40, 42
Grainau 50, 62, 85
Grieg, Edvard 7
Grosvenor Gallery 6
Grove, Sir George 87-88

Hammersbach 49-50, 54, 83, *84*, 85, 87
Harwich 10, 18
Hasfield Court 7, 35
Heidelberg 11, 14-17
Hereford 88
Herkomer, Hubert von front cover, 2, 5-6, *6*
Hoch Alp 54, 85
Hollenthal 50, 61
Holzer, Johann E 52
Hook of Holland 10, 18

Immenstadt 33-34, 42
Innsbruck 18, 20-21, 57, 59-60
Interlaken 16

Johannes, B *53*, 53

Kaprun 21
Karwendel 59
Kitzbühel 21
Kleinwalsertal 41

Landsberg 5
Leeds
    Choral Union 87
    Mercury 88

Index

Leicester, Hubert 3, 17, 36
Leipzig 3
Lermoos 60
Letts, Charles & Co 4
Leutasch Tal 59
Lindau 11, 14, *15*, 17, 42
Linz 19
Longfellow, H W 16
Ludwig, King of Bavaria 30-31
Mainz 11, 17
Malvern 6, 30-31, 36, 87
   Forli 7, 9, 30
Manns, August 4, 87
Margate 16
Mary, Queen 49
Mascagni : *Cavalleria Rusticana* 25
Mendelssohn, Felix 16
Minim, The 53, *53*
Mittenwald 21, 50, 59-60
Mittleberg 41
Mozart, Wolfgang 20
   Don Giovanni 32
Munich 1, 5, 8, 11-12, 14, 17-18, 22-33, 42, 48, 62-63, 71, 73, 81
   Alte Pinakothek *25*, 25, 30-31
   Konigliches Hof *24*, 26
   Nymphenberg Palace 30
   Residenz, Die 31
Murnau 54, 83, 86, 90
Musical Times, The 89

Nassereit 60
Nevinson, Basil 9
Novello & Co 9, 15-16, 75, 78-80
Nuremberg 11, 13-14, 34

Oberammergau 57-59, 64, 71
Oberau 59
Obermoos 60
Oberstdorf 1, 11, 14, 23, 33-41, 73
   Loretto Chapels *38-39*, 39-40
   Rathaus 34, *37*
Ostend 10, 17-18
Oytal Valley 40-41, *rear cover*

Paris 10, 22
Partenkirchen 43-44, 49-50, 51-52, 85, 87
Partnachklamm 59
Passau 19
Penny, Dora - see Powell, Mrs Richard
Powell, Mrs Richard 8, 15, 81-82, 87
Prendergast, H D 51

Queenborough 10

Regensburg 19
Richter, Hans 4, 16
Riessersee 54, 82

Sachs, Hans 13-14, 29, 31
St Anton 49, 51, 53-54, *56*, 82, 85, 87
St Gilgen 20
St Wolfgang 20
Salzburg 20
Schmutzer, Josef 45, 52
Schöll, Martin 65
Schöllang 41
Schuhplättler 47, 76 & *front cover*
Schumann, Robert 16
Seealpsee 40
Seefeld 21, 59, 60
Slingsby-Bethell family 1, 49, 51, 54, 57, 61, 63, 65, 68, *69*, 71, 73, 75
Sonnenbichl 50, 82, *83*
Southampton 5
Staffelsee 54
Starnberger See 31
Stillach Valley 42
Stockley, William 4
Strand Magazine, The 3
Strasbourg 21-22
Strauss, Richard 32, 48
   Alpine Symphony 48

Three Choirs Festival 4, 9
Trench, Mary 58
Tubingen 16

Uhland, Ludwig 16

Wagner 3-4, 6, 8, 12, 23, 26-28, 30-32, 42, 71, 81
   Flying Dutchman, The 3, 31-32
   Götterdämmerung 26, 31
   Lohengrin 3
   Meistersingers, Die 4, 8, 12, 26, 31
   Parsifal 3, 8, 12-13, 75
   Rheingold, Das 26
   Seigfried 26
   Tannhäuser 3, 4, 26-27
   Tristan und Isolde 8, 12, 26, 32, 57
   Walkure, Die 4, 26
Walserschanzle 41
Wamberg 50, 83, *84*, 85
Waxenstein 61
West Kensington 7
Wetterstein 48, 61
Williams, Joseph 75, 79-80, 86
Wilton, Lord 49
Worcester 80, 86
   St George's Church 36
   Festival Choral Society 86
Worcestershire Philharmonic Society 26, 88
Wurzburg 19

Zugspitze 48, 60, 82
Zwingsteg 41

Also from Elgar Editions
The Best of Me -
A Gerontius Centenary Companion

The apocryphal history of Gerontius is well known - how Elgar's late completion of the vocal score, the Birmingham choirmaster's untimely death and the failure of his replacement to appreciate the complexity of the work led to an under-rehearsed première which the critics panned. Fortunately, a German choirmaster in the audience recognised the work's considerable merits and arranged a subsequent performance in Dusseldorf which single-handedly rescued the work from oblivion. But how accurate is this snapshot? What followed Düsseldorf? How widely accepted is the oratorio today? And how important was the poem to Newman's reputation before Elgar chose to set it?

The Best of Me is the first book to attempt to provide a complete history of Gerontius, tracing the work's fortunes through a mixture of contemporary reviews and retrospective analyses from a biographical portrait of Newman and his writing of the epic poem to a final chapter which reviews the status Gerontius has achieved in the world today. The text is supplemented by some ninety illustrations and additional material from a variety of sources. With contributors including Elgar biographer Michael Kennedy, eminent musicologist Lewis Foreman and a number of leading authorities from within the Elgar Society, this is a book that should interest the academic and the general reader alike, a pleasure to read as well as a valuable reference source.

To purchase the book, or to obtain further details, visit the Elgar Society's website [*http://www.elgar.org/7ebest.htm*] or write to :

Elgar Editions, 20 High Street, Rickmansworth, Herts WD3 1ER

384 pages with 90 illustrations   ISBN 0 9537082 0 9   RRP £ 18.00

Front cover : Schuhplattler, from a painting by Hubert von Herkomer
[Neues Stadtmuseum, Landsberg am Lech]

Back cover : The Oytal valley   [J W Greaves]